Published by North West Fine
Foods Limited, Skelmersdale
Editor and Author, Sue Nelson
Foreword, Simon Rimmer

Book design by cellcreative
Printed and bound in North
West England on Revive 100

ISBN 978-0-9555095-0-6

Contents

Foreword

by Simon Rimmer

Since accidently becoming a chef at Greens in Didsbury some years ago, I have never looked back or regretted my move into the food industry. It isn't easy opening or running a restaurant, you need a clear vision and to stick to your plan. Through tough times I have been motivated to succeed by the fine food producers that surround me in the North West. They are dedicated, hardworking and deserve success.

Like many chefs, I am passionate about the ingredients I use and you too can become a better cook overnight, by simply using and supporting the many great regional food producers that we have in the North West. The taste difference is clearly evident. Take time to source quality local and regional food whenever possible. By doing so, not only do you get to eat good food that has a traceable origin, but you get back in touch with farmers and food producers in your locality, just as our ancestors did. You will also learn when things are in season and at their best and what is good value for money.

I use many of the producers that are featured in this book for the ingredients that I buy for my restaurants, and to cook at home for my family. Spend time sourcing local produce. I think it's well worth it - you will too.

Simon Rimmer
Patron, NW Fine Food

Introduction

NW Fine Food
is a membership
organisation. All
our members are
producers from the
North West who each
own a £5 share in the
company. We don't
make a profit and any
money we make is
ploughed back into
developing their
businesses - promoting
them, helping them
grow and generally
trying to sell more
of their local produce.

I have had the wonderful pleasure of meeting these producers and hearing their very personal stories. And believe me, all of them have a great story to tell. Take Michelle, who used to work in the smoothie bar at Harvey Nicks in Manchester. Obsessed by pickles, chutneys and apples, (trust me they're all like this!), she left her beloved job, researched the market for a year and started Clippy's Apple Preserves.

She is determined to protect our native North West apple orchards, and works with a range of local orchards and suppliers. The passion for her work shines through in everything she does, and her delicious preserves include the magnificent Apple and Rhubarb Jam. All her products are handmade in small batches with a big dollop of Clippy love. Just a typical NW Fine Food member really.

Then there is Farmersharp: Andrew and Stuart supply beef, lamb, mutton and a range of charcuterie from their base in Lindal-in-Furness in Cumbria. You cannot find a more vocal supporter than Nigel Haworth (of Michelin-starred Northcote Manor), when it comes to their three week hung mutton. Nigel is so adamant that it is 'simply the best' he even took some to France to prove to his continental counterparts how good it was. Needless to say, they too were absolutely convinced.

We also have producers who are true family businesses: Edge & Son have been butchers, producing rare breed and organic meats in the Wirral since the 1800s. So too have Gordon and Gillian Clark's family in Penrith and Frank Taylor's family in Sale.

Richard Woodall Ltd in Millom, Cumbria, have a royal warrant to supply H.M. Queen Elizabeth II with Cumberland sausages. The company is still in family hands and they were established in 1828.

Bartons Pickles in St Helens, make the definitive piccalilli (in my opinion) and have done so for over a hundred years. Eddisbury Fruit Farm have been growing fruit and vegetables from their rich Cheshire soils since 1936. Amanda Dowson's family have farmed in the Ribble Valley since 1954, producing cream and milk and some delicious ice cream from their Hostein herd. Freda Neale's ancestors have been farming in the heart of rural Lancashire for so long they can't tell you when it all started, but they now sell their farm produce from a rather good farm shop. I could go on and on.

Not one of our members is boring or dispassionate, because to make, rear or grow your own products is not for the faint hearted when you consider the power of the competition. What they make is often the result of generations of work - recipes handed down, animals looked after, fruit and veg lovingly cared for. If you talk to them they're open and honest about the way they create the end product. The big boys might have hijacked all the marketing phrases but if you rely on your senses, you can smell, see and (ha ha) taste the difference.

I really hope you find this guide useful and informative, but if you want to truly help the fabulous producers in this book, you need to make the effort to source these products every now and then. Time is always in short supply, but making the effort, say once a month, to go to a farmshop or farmers' market to stock up, will help sustain the heritage and hard work involved in local production. If you can't manage that, become a NW Fine Food Lover member, go to www.nwfinefood.co.uk and find out more.

I'm very proud to be living and working in the North West, and I challenge you to buy something local and see what all the fuss is about.

Happy eating

Sue Nelson
Chief Executive
NW Fine Food

nwfinefoodawards
2007

Every year NW Fine Food
hold their annual awards
to recognise the best in fine
food from Cumbria, Cheshire,
Greater Manchester,
Merseyside and Lancashire.
It is free to enter, and we
encourage all producers,
whether they are our members
or not, to send in their top
three products. Encouragingly
every year we receive
hundreds and hundreds
of entries from the region.

In all there are fifty categories ranging from chocolate to chutneys, pies to puddings and sausages to soups. Our esteemed panel of judges get together for a full day of tastings; debating and arguing their way through to a final decision on each of the categories.

Logistically, it's not easy for us to organise. We have to make sure the deliveries are received over a two day period and that they are kept in the best condition. The cheeses must be taken out of the fridge at the right time to ensure they are being tasted at optimum temperature. Ice creams need to remain frozen until the last minute. Sausages need to be cooked, meat prepared, bread baked and so on.

The tastings are carried out 'blind'. That is to say all packaging is removed and each food item numbered so that they cannot be identified. The panels use a marking sheet to judge how it looks, and most importantly to assess its taste and texture. After a full day of debate we decide on the winners for each of the 50 categories, and you will find them here in this book.

After the 50 category winners are announced, we then decide on the best product for each of the region's five counties, and we name the best new product of 2007. But the ultimate accolade is our overall winner who is crowned "NW Fine Food Producer of the Year 2007".

If you have a family gathering, a dinner party, you need an unusual present or you simply want to indulge yourself, you really should try the examples shown in this book. While you're out shopping look out for the distinctive "NW Fine Food Award 2007 Winner" labels, and see if you agree with our judges.

The judges

We would like to thank the following people, who gave up their time to be judges for the NW Fine Food Awards 2007. Held on the 21 February at Blackburn Rovers FC, it's a tough job but someone's got to do it!

Alison Seagrave Harvey Nichols
David Gale Selfridges
Emily Shamma Tesco
Hannah Waring Booths
James Dodds Asda
James Fisher Marks & Spencer
Mike Spragg Harvey Nichols
Phil Godwin Booths
Robbie James Waitrose

Annette Gibbons Food writer
Beverley Paul Food journalist
Catherine Owens Northern Life
Claire Sherwin Cumbria Life
Emma Sturgis Metro
Gillian Cowburn Westmorland Gazette
Jonathan Schofield City Life,
Radio Manchester
Louise Taylor Pure Taste
Mark Green Carlisle News and Star
Mark Holdstock Farming Today
Matthew Fort The Target and The Guardian
Ruth Allen Manchester Evening News,
The Independent
William Grieves The Daily Telegraph

Anthony McGrath Catering Connection
Gary Manning 60 Hope Street
Gordon Clark Restaurant Association
Julie Bagnoli Isinglass Dining Rooms
Malcolm Large Seafish
Mark Bennett Maimaison
Martin Ainscough The Raquet Club
Martin Smith Manchester University
Matthew Worsley NW Fine Food Young
Chef of the Year 2006
Nigel Haworth Northcote Manor,
The Three Fishes
Paddy Byrne Everyman Bistro
Paul Askew London Carriage Works
Roger Ward Sam's Chop House
Simon Radley Chester Grosvenor
Steven Doherty First Floor Café, Lakeland

Keith Blundell Liverpool Culture Company
Krys Zasada Manchester Markets
Nick Brooks-Sykes
Northwest Development Agency
Pam Wilsher The Mersey Partnership
Thom Hetherington Moorfield Media

nwfinefood
new product of the year 2007

LIZZIE'S HOME MADE
Cumbrian Frutta Cotta Mostarda

Awarded to a product which was not on sale before January 2006. We are keen to encourage product innovation, and to get producers to continue to look to the future as well as drawing on the best traditions of the past. Mostarda is based on the traditional, voluptuous Italian condiment of fruit preserved in syrup that gains a kick from the addition of mustard. It's traditionally served with boiled meats in northern Italy. Lizzie makes hers from the finest ingredients and they all come through in the taste. You just have to buy it because, as one of our judges said, "it's a winner".

Elizabeth Smith
Lizzie's Home Made, The Bank, Dockray, Matterdale, Penrith, Cumbria CA11 0LG
phone 01768 482487
www.fruttacotta.co.uk

Availability: Retail and wholesale, the website details available stockists.

nwfinefood
producer of the year 2007

PORT OF LANCASTER SMOKEHOUSE
Naturally Smoked Boneless Kipper

This really is the top accolade that any of our producers could wish to achieve in 2007. Not only does it recognise the high quality of their products, but they need to be openly passionate about what they do, enthuse their staff so they act as ambassadors and base their businesses around quality and provenance. Established over thirty years ago, the Port of Lancaster Smokehouse has retained the traditional methods of preparing and curing fish and meats. You can tell they're thoroughly commited to the quality of their products, especially in the ingredients they use, which are sourced as locally as possible.

They smoke salmon, haddock, trout, eel, ham, bacon, duck, chicken and game, and you can even bring in your own products that they'll smoke for you. But it's the outstanding Naturally Smoked Boneless Kipper that has won them the prestigious Producer of the Year 2007 accolade. The judges were unanimous in their praise for the moistness and flavour of their smoked kipper. As one judge put it, "luscious visually with wonderful texture, subtle flavour and beautiful skin".

Michael Price
Port of Lancaster Smokehouse, West Quay, Glasson Dock, Nr Lancaster, Lancashire LA2 0DB
phone 01524 751493
www.glassonsmokehouse.co.uk

Availability: At food events and local farmers' markets, mail order online and own factory shop.

The finest food in the North West

Dairy

Bakery and confectionery

Meat

Fish

Beverages

Chutneys and preserves

Prepared foods

Fresh produce

Dairy

Cheese
Yogurt
Ice cream
Sorbet

nwfinefood awards 2007

Best DAIRY PRODUCT and Best BLUE CHEESE

Dew-Lay
Garstang Blue

The best dairy product includes all cheese categories, ice cream, sorbets and yogurt. Of all those tasted the judges were unanimous that Garstang Blue was the overall winner, seeing off stiff competition particularly in the other cheese categories. For the Best Blue Cheese, judges were looking for a complex cheese, which was moist with a lingering flavour and a number of tastes bursting in the mouth. To qualify it must be made in the region and should use regional ingredients. Dew-Lay have been makers of award winning cheeses since 1957 using locally sourced milk. This cheese is complex with a deep yellow ochre colour, sticky and moist, and was described by one judge as "excellent, with a nutty flavour".

Ian Coggin
Dew-Lay, Garstang, Preston, Lancashire PR3 0PR
phone 01995 602335
www.dewlay.com

Availability: Available from cheese shops and many national supermarket chains.

Notes on cheese

One of the things I love most about cheese is its tradition and history, and the fact that someone has taken months and sometimes even years making it for me. To store it I need to keep it chilled and moist and to eat it, I need do nothing more than slowly bring it to room temperature - real convenience food.

Great cheese is complex and sophisticated. It should have a relatively high fat content, which begins to melt and coat your tongue as you eat it. If it's spectacularly good, when it melts the flavour should linger and there should be a number of tastes bursting in your mouth. If the flavour stops half way down your tongue, the cheese is of poor quality and has probably been over-chilled, made quickly and matured in plastic wrapping.

There are four types of cheese that are superb in the North West and are worth seeking out. The first and most obvious is hard cheese, and in particular, Lancashire. It's been made from at least the 13th Century - only takes two months or so to mature, it's creamy when young and crumbly when more mature with a buttery salty twang. It is without doubt the number one cooking cheese, especially for slowly grilled hot melty cheese on toast. There are some great blue cheeses in the North West too, which can be gritty, rough, dry or sticky in texture, and can come in a variety of colours.

We are also becoming very good at making soft cheese, the equivalent to French brie. This has a white fuzzy rind and just stops short of being runny. The best have a mushroom taste and a hint of sherry (honest!). Natural rind cheeses, which are usually goat's cheese are also becoming popular with cheesemakers. When young they're moist with a hint of lemon, but as they age they develop a fine bluish grey mould, become drier and look a bit more wrinkly, with a sophisticated nutty flavour.

Alston Dairy Ltd

Ann Forshaw
Alston, Longridge, Preston,
Lancashire PR3 3BN
phone 01772 782621
email ann@alstondairy.co.uk
www.alstondairy.co.uk

Availability: Available from supermarkets and other food outlets, both across the North West and the UK.

Description: A family business run by dairy farmers using established recipes and finest ingredients including milk from their own Friesian herd. They produce seven different types of yoghurt in thirty different flavours. They are justly proud of the many awards they have received.

Brades Farm Dairy

John & April Towers
Brades Farm, Farleton, Lancaster,
Lancashire LA2 9LF
phone 01524 221589
email
enquiries@bradesfarm.co.uk
www.bradesfarm.co.uk

Availability: Available locally by doorstep delivery, and from food outlets around Lancashire.

Description: Situated in the Lune Valley, Brades Farm specialise in producing fully traceable milk products and cream from their own dairy herd. The milk is processed and packaged on the farm, then delivered direct to local customers. Suppliers to retailers, eating establishments and the milk bottle doorstep trade.

Butlers Farmhouse Cheeses

Neil Meredith
Wilson Fields Farm, Inglewhite,
Preston, Lancashire PR3 2LH
phone 01772 781500
email sales@butlerscheeses.co.uk
www.butlerscheeses.co.uk

Availability: Widely available from cheese shops, fine food outlets, restaurants and supermarkets across the UK.

Description: Traditionally handmade farmhouse cheeses including Lancashires, Red Leicester, Double Gloucester, Cheshire, Wensleydale, Cheddar and the famous Blacksticks Blue. Made in open vats to traditional recipes. Most are round, hand bound and waxed. Slowly matured and turned by hand.

Carron Lodge

David Williams
Park Head Farm, Inglewhite,
Preston, Lancashire PR3 2LN
tel 01995 640352

Availability: Widely available from food retailers throughout the North West and the UK, please call for further details.

Description: All products are made with non-animal rennet and are GM free, and include Farmhouse Butter, Lancashire Blue, Inglewhite Goats Cheese, Inglewhite Sheep's Cheese and home produced Oak-smoked Cheese to mention but a few.

nwfinefoodawards 2007

Thornby Moor Dairy
Tovey (Goats Cheese)

Best SOFT CHEESE

To qualify the cheese must be made in the region and should use regional ingredients. Judges were looking for good aging, medium dryness with a sophisticated nutty flavour that lingers. Matthew Fort of The Guardian, summed up the general comments – "a good cheese. Well made". Thornby Moor Dairy is run by Carolyn and Leonie Fairbairn. Carolyn began making cheeses in 1979, using milk from goats, sheep and cows. Their milk is sourced from single herds "to capture the essence of Cumbria in the flavours of our cheeses". They've certainly succeeded with Tovey.

Leonie Fairbairn
Thornby Moor Dairy, Crofton Hall, Thursby, Carlisle, Cumbria CA5 6QB
phone 01697 345555
www.churchmousecheeses.com

Availability: Visits by appointment or order online.

Cheshire Farm Ice Cream

Sally Poulter
Drumlan Hall, Newton Lane,
Tattenhall, Chester,
Cheshire CH3 9NE
phone 01829 770995
email
enquiries@cheshirefarmicecream.co.uk
www.cheshirefarmicecream.co.uk

Availability: Available from their own ice cream parlour, and from retailers throughout Cheshire and the North West.

Description: This award winning real dairy ice cream is made with fresh whole milk and fresh cream and uses only the finest ingredients with natural flavourings and colourings. Cheshire Farm Real Dairy Ice Cream and Real Fruit Sorbet are available in over 30 refreshingly different flavours with additional seasonal specials in a wide range of packaging sizes to suit all requirements.

Cringlebrook

Philip & Carla Battarbee
Cringlebrook Farm, Ashley Lane,
Goosnargh, Preston,
Lancashire PR3 2EE
phone 01772 865279

Availability: Available at farmers' markets and from good cheese shops and on restaurant cheese boards in the region.

Description: Traditional handmade goats cheese, made from the Battarbee's own goats milk. The cheese is hard pressed to give it a firm creamy texture. It is then ripened, as mild and creamy or mature (naturally mould ripened).

Cumberland Dairy Ltd

Christopher Johnston
and Kevin Beaty
Knock Cross, Long Marton,
Appleby, Cumbria CA16 6DT
phone 01768 88776
email
info@cumberlanddairy.co.uk
www.thecumberlanddairy.co.uk

Availability: Available at Cranston's Food Hall and JJ Graham in Penrith, at Booths and from good cheese shops throughout the region. Visit the website for a full list of stockists.

Description: The Cumberland Dairy was formed by a group of dairy farmers in Cumbria in 2004 - they are passionate about their farms and their idyllic rural landscape. The cheeses are made to farmhouse recipes in a traditional farmhouse creamery and have won both Gold and Silver medals at the British Cheese Awards.

Cumbrian Maid

Sheila & Grahame Latus
Bonaly, 4 Lonsdale Terrace, Penrith, Cumbria CA11 7TS
phone 01768 890538

Availability: Available at farmers' markets and food events across the region.

Description: Producers of fantastic low fat frozen yogurt which is blended with a selection of home grown fruits and wild blackberries gathered on Cumbrian Fells. No pesticides or artificial fertilisers are used.

nwfinefood awards 2007

Best HARD CHEESE

Dew-Lay
Creamy Lancashire

To qualify the cheese must be made in the region and should use regional ingredients. Judges were looking for depth of flavour with a buttery taste. Dew-Lay have been makers of award winning cheeses since 1957 using locally sourced milk. The Lancashire cheese range also includes Crumbly, Tasty and Special Reserve.

Judges comments included "super taste and texture" and "all round a great cheese. Excellent!"

Ian Coggin
Dew-Lay, Garstang, Preston, Lancashire PR3 0PR
phone 01995 602335
www.dewlay.com

Availability: Available from cheese shops and many national supermarket chains.

Delamere Dairy Ltd

Liz Sutton
Yew Tree Farm, Bexton Lane,
Knutsford, Cheshire WA16 9BH
phone 01565 632422
email info@delameredairy.co.uk
www.delameredairy.co.uk

Availability: Available from supermarkets throughout the UK.

Description: Producers of a delicious range of goats milk based dairy products, including milk, yogurts, butter and a selection of cheeses. All products are made using pasteurised milk from welfare assured goat herds.

Dew-Lay

Ian Coggin
Garstang, Preston,
Lancashire PR3 0PR
phone 01995 602335
email ian@dewlay.com
www.dewlay.com

Availability: Available from cheese shops and many national supermarket chains.

Description: Makers of award winning cheeses since 1957 using locally sourced milk. The Lancashire cheese range includes Creamy, Crumbly, Tasty, Special Reserve and the wonderful Garstang Blue. The business also operates a cutting and packing plant where they can cut, slice and grate cheese to suit customer's needs.

Dowsons Dairies Ltd

Amanda Dowson
Hawkshaw Farm, Longsight Road,
Clayton-le-Dale, Blackburn,
Lancashire BB2 7JA
phone 01254 812407
email info@mrsdowsons.co.uk
www.mrsdowsons.co.uk

Availability: Available from a
variety of outlets across the region,
please call for further details.

Description: The Dowson family
have farmed the lush pastures
of the Ribble Valley since 1954,
producing milk and cream, as
well as the fabulous Mrs Dowsons
Real Dairy Ice Cream, made using
the milk and cream from their own
Holstein herd and the very best
flavour ingredients available.

Dunham Massey Farm Ice Cream

Ann Pennington
and Dianne Ogden
Ash Farm, Station Road,
Dunham Massey, Nr Altrincham,
Cheshire WA14 5SG
phone 0161 928 1230

Availability: Available from their
farm shop and from food shows
and farmers' markets across the
region, including Ashton Farmers'
Market and the Manchester Fine
Foods Markets.

Description: A mother and
daughter partnership producing
20 flavours of ice-cream.
Undoubtedly a luxury product
hand made with double cream
and whole milk.

nwfinefoodawards
2007

Pakeeza
Lancashire Farm Wholemilk Set Probiotic Yoghurt

Best
YOGHURT

To qualify the yogurt must be made in the region and should use regional ingredients. Yoghurt is traditionally made by pouring cultured milk into pots to ferment, set and become creamy.
The taste should combine this creaminess with a sourness from the lactose acid produced. Judges described this as a "good, natural, true product". Pakeeza Dairies was established in 1982 by the Zouq family. They have won a number of other prizes for this yogurt at the Nantwich International Cheese Show and the Great Yorkshire Show.

Elaine Burke
Pakeeza, Kingsway West Business Park,
Mossbridge Road, Rochdale,
Lancashire OL16 5LX
phone 01706 641551
www.pakeeza.co.uk

Availability: Through independent retail stores across the UK.

English Lakes Ice Cream

Peter Fryer
The Old Dairy, Gilthwaiterigg Lane,
Kendal, Cumbria LA9 6NT
phone 01539 721211
www.lakesicecream.com

Availability: Available from their shop at the Old Dairy, and from outlets throughout Cumbria, the North West, and nationally.

Description: Made in Kendal with the deep passion for their product evident in every spoonful. They are recognised as producers of luxury dairy ice cream and real fruit sorbets, including winning North West Fine Food Awards in 2001, 2003 and 2004 for their ice cream.

Hartleys Ice Cream

Mark Richardson
24 Church Street, Egremont,
Cumbria CA22 2AW
phone 01946 820456
www.hartleys-icecream.co.uk

Availability: Available from The Creamery, from The Ice Cream Parlour and Coffee Shop or the Beach Shop and Cafe at the sea front on Beach Road in St. Bees.

Description: Producers of over 25 flavours of ice cream and sorbet from traditional family recipes. All their ice creams and sorbets are homemade at the creamery in Egremont.

Holwood Cheese

Andy & Lisa Walling
Hallidays Farm, Bilsborrow, Preston,
Lancashire PR3 0RU
phone 01995 640325

Availability: Available from
cheese shops and farmers'
markets throughout the region.

Description: Established at the
Walling's farm and dairy, situated in
the heart of the Fylde countryside,
Holwood only use milk from their
farm assured herd of pedigree
Holsteins, giving total traceability
from cow to consumer. Traditionally
hand made with rennet suitable
for vegetarians and GM free.

Huntley's - Moo 2 You

Eddie Cowpe
Huntley Gate Farm,
Whalley Road, Samlesbury,
Preston, Lancashire PR5 0UN
phone 01772 877309
www.huntleys.co.uk

Availability: Available from their
farm shop and Harvey Nichols
and other fine food retailers in
the North West.

Description: Moo 2 You ice
cream is made with the freshest
milk and cream from Huntley's
own cows. This delicious ice
cream won two Great Taste
Awards in 2005 and Huntley's itself
won the 2006 Lancashire and
Blackpool Tourism Award for 'Rural
Tourism Retailer of the Year'.

Notes on ice cream

Ice cream evokes so many memories of childhood, something that was a real treat on a day out, or even to be taken when you were ill, and couldn't manage to eat anything else.

In its simplest form ice cream is just flavoured and frozen cream, but it's depressing to realise that most of the major producers of ice cream, make a product that contains no cream at all. If you look at the labels you'll see they're often non-dairy products, that don't even contain milk. The fat, which is essential in making ice cream is from vegetable oil or even animal fat, and if there is milk, it is in powdered form. So called 'value' ice cream, isn't value for money at all, as you are paying for the huge amount of air that is whisked into it.

When searching for the real thing, buy 'dairy ice cream', this guarantees that the fats are all dairy. The finest though, is made with whole milk and double cream, and sometimes with egg or egg yolk added. The North West produces some of the best examples with the lush grass in the region ideal for cows to produce premium milk.

Ice cream should have a smooth firm texture and a rich creamy, fresh, clean taste, and not be full of tiny tasteless icy particles, or be too sweet or eggy. The feel of the frozen product, sliding across your tongue and hitting the back of your throat on a very hot summer's day, will be invigorating and cooling at the same time. Vanilla is by far the most popular variety, and it is here you can tell if it's really good, as it doesn't mask the quality of the ice cream itself. However, there are also some wonderful examples of flavoured ice creams too, using fruit, nuts or the finest chocolate, although these should be understated in flavour.

nwfinefoodawards
2007

Best
VANILLA ICE
CREAM

Cater 4
Vanilla

To qualify the ice cream must be made in the region and should use regional ingredients, preferably whole milk and double cream. It should have a smooth firm texture and a rich creamy, fresh, clean taste and not be too sweet or eggy. The vanilla flavour shouldn't mask the quality of the ice cream itself. This wonderful ice cream has been created by Andrew and Nicola Bowker of Cater 4 and satisfied all the judges stringent criteria, beating a number of well established award winning competitors.

Dudley Carruthers
Cater 4, Schola Green Lane, Morecambe, Lancashire LA4 5QS
phone 01524 411611
www.fellbred.co.uk

Availability: Available by mail order online.

Mrs Kirkhams Lancashire Cheese

Graham Kirkham
Beesley Farm, Mill Lane,
Goosnargh, Preston,
Lancashire PR3 2FL
phone 01772 865335
email graham@mrskirkhams.com
www.mrskirkhams.com

Availability: Widely available from good cheese shops, delis, and on restaurant menus. Also at farmers' markets and food events, check their website for further information.

Description: The Kirkham family have been making traditional farmhouse Lancashire cheese for the past 25 years. They have achieved numerous awards, the most prestigious being 'Supreme Champion' at the British Cheese Show. They use only their own milk to produce a selection of individually handcrafted unpasteurised cheeses.

Leagram Organic Dairy

Robert & Faye Kitching
High Head Farm Buildings,
Moss Lane, Chipping, Preston,
Lancashire PR3 2NR
phone 01995 61532
email
info@cheese-experience.com
www.cheese-experience.com

Availability: Available direct from the farm, at farmers' markets and from good cheese shops and delis throughout the region.

Description: Manufacturer of organic cow and sheep milk cheeses produced from local milk in the Trough of Bowland. Treated gently to produce a cheese of character and quality. Five different types plus many additive cheeses sold on site and at local shops. They also have a viewing area so that you may watch it being made.

Lewis Brothers Ice Cream

Emma Brierley
Lewis Square, Lilford Street,
Warrington, Cheshire WA5 5LJ
phone 01925 632994

Availability: Available by the scoop at outlets across the region, please call for further details.

Description: Manufacturers of premium Italian ice cream in a large range of exciting flavours, made to a 100 year old traditional recipe, using the finest ingredients and natural flavours. Gelato di Parma is packed either for scoop ice cream or catering use. They also manufacture liquid ice cream mix and wholesale all items to accompany ice cream.

Little Town Dairy Ltd

Janet Forshaw
Chipping Road, Thornley, Preston,
Lancashire PR3 2TB
phone 01772 782429

Availability: Available from food retailers both regionally and nationally.

Description: Manufacturers of quality award winning dairy products including yoghurts, crème fraiche, soured cream and probiotic yoghurt drinks. All products are made from their own milk from a freedom food accredited herd.

nwfinefoodawards 2007

English Lakes Ice Cream
Raspberry Pavlova

Best
FLAVOURED
ICE CREAM

To qualify the ice cream must be made in the region and should use regional ingredients, preferably whole milk and double cream. It should have a smooth firm texture and a rich creamy, fresh, clean taste. English Lakes Ice Cream is based in Kendal and have won NW Fine Food Awards before, in 2001, 2003 and 2004. Judges really enjoyed this ice cream describing it as having a "good raspberry flavour".

Peter Fryer
English Lakes Ice Cream, The Old Dairy, Gilthwaiterigg Lane, Kendal, Cumbria LA9 6NT
phone 01539 721211
www.lakesicecream.com

Availability: Available from their shop at the Old Dairy, and from outlets throughout Cumbria, the North West and nationally.

JJ Sandham Ltd

Chris Sandham
Rostock Dairy,
Garstang Road, Barton, Preston,
Lancashire PR3 5AA
phone 01995 640247

Availability: Available
from cheese shops and
retailers nationally.

Description: Manufacturers of
traditional Lancashire cheese
since 1929. Available in Mild,
Tasty and Crumbly also with garlic,
sage and smoked. Two varieties
of organic Lancashire cheese also
produced. All cheeses are hand
made from pasteurised milk using
vegetarian, GMO free rennet.

Singleton's Dairy

Stuart Robinson
Mill Farm, Preston Road,
Longridge, Preston,
Lancashire PR3 3AN
phone 01772 782112
email quality@singletons.uk.com
www.singletons.uk.com

Availability: Widely available
from cheese shops, supermarkets
and food retailers both regionally
and nationally.

Description: Singleton's Beacon
Fell Lancashire Cheese has a
much coveted Protection of
Designated Origin status, ensuring
the cheese can only come from
within a five mile radius of Brecon
Fell. Strict rules say that the milk
must come from within this area
and the traditional two and three
days curd method is property of
this local farming community.

AD&PE Shorrock

Andrew & Pauline Shorrock
Newhouse Farm, Ford Lane,
Goosnargh, Preston,
Lancashire PR3 2FJ
phone 01772 865250
www.northernharvest.co.uk

Availability: Available direct
from the farm and from farmers'
markets and food events
throughout the North West.
Also available online.

Description: Traditional
handmade Lancashire cheese
following methods and recipes
handed down from three
generations of the Shorrock family.
Cheeses available include Tasty
Lancashire, Mild Lancashire,
flavoured Lancashires and Black
Beauty Bomb - a strong creamy
Lancashire encased in its own
waxed jacket.

Tiresford Guernsey Gold

Andrew Hope
Tiresford Farm, Tarporley,
Cheshire CW6 9LY
phone 01829 734080
www.tggcheshireyogurt.co.uk

Availability: Available from food
outlets in Cheshire, please visit
the website for further details.

Description: Milk from the
prize winning "Tiresford" herd of
pedigree Guernsey cows is used
to produce a live Cheshire-
branded yoghurt of the very
highest quality which is distributed
to local outlets on the day of
production using their own
refrigerated transport.

David Williams Cheese

David Williams
9-11 The Square, Sandbach,
Cheshire CW11 1AP
phone 01270 762817

Availability: Available on site from their delicatessen.

Description: Manufacturers of specialist cheeses, they have been blending additive cheeses since 1993 and have won many prizes at international cheese shows. Bowland, Bradburys Wholenut and Red Hot Mex are some of the cheeses they manufacture. They also produce cheese baskets and gift packs all year round.

Windermere Ice Cream Co Ltd

Steven Duffin
Unit 3, Back Ellerthwaite Road,
Windermere, Cumbria LA23 2AL
phone 01539 447876
www.windermereicecream.co.uk

Availability: Available by the scoop from numerous shops around Cumbria, please visit the website for a full list. Chocolates also available online.

Description: From the beautiful Windermere area in the Lake District, Windermere Ice Cream produce 32 flavours of ice cream and sorbets and the unique (and wonderful) damson gin chocolates.

nwfinefoodawards 2007

Frederick's Ice Cream
Sangria Sorbet

To qualify the sorbet must be made in the region using regional ingredients where possible. Sorbets are basically a mixture of water, sugar and fruit juice. They should be silky smooth and make your mouth tingle. The judges were impressed by the flavour, texture and colour, particularly picking up the citrus twang. Fredericks have been making award winning ice cream and sorbets in the Chorley area since 1892 and are proud of their Italian roots.

Donna Townson
Frederick's Ice Cream, Bolton Road, Charnock, Chorley, Lancashrie PR7 4AZ
phone 01257 263154
www.fredericksicecream.co.uk

Availability: Supplied to the trade and through their own ice cream parlours and mobile vendors.

Best
SORBET

Bakery and confectionery

Cakes
Puddings
Sweet pastries
Bread
Biscuits
Confectionery

nwfinefoodawards 2007

Best BAKERY OR CONFECTIONERY and Best BREAD

Munx Lakeland Bakery
Cumbrian Honey Bread with Fig

The Best Bakery and Confectionery category includes cakes, puddings, sweet pastries, biscuits and confectionery. Munx Lakeland Bakery won the overall award for its Cumbrian Honey Bread with Fig. Not only did it taste fabulous but it looked wonderful too. It was described by judges as "very, very good", "a winner" and having a "good figgy taste and good crust". Like all good bakery or confectionery products it smelt delicious. Munx Lakeland Bakery is an independent baker producing traditional bread, speciality bread and patisserie using the finest ingredients and craftsmanship. Their passion for the art of bread making was evident in this category award winner.

Aidan Monks and Sara Hall
Munx Lakeland Bakery, 9-11 Mill Yard, Staveley, Kendal, Cumbria LA8 9LR
phone 01539 822102

Availability: Available from the bakery at Staveley and from food outlets throughout Cumbria and North Lancashire. Please call for further details.

Notes on bread

Bread is a simple, honest and satisfying staple of life.

At least it should be. It has been made by man for thousands of years without being adulterated, however the invention of the white sliced loaf, has led to a chemically laden, mass produced product that is a million miles away from the real thing. Instead of a slow process where the dough is stretched and matured, kept warm so that it rises and then baked, it is beaten quickly, rises using additives and baked, all within the hour.

Decent bread can be bought in farmers' markets or farm shops, or you can easily make your own, where the end product smells delicious, does not crumble when it's sliced, retains a chewiness to it and a texture that can absorb a spread of butter not collapse under its weight.

Whilst sliced bread sales are huge, uncut loaves taste so much better, especially for toast, and the extra effort of cutting is well worth it. Speciality breads abound, with added nuts, seeds, sun-dried tomatoes, herbs, cheese, olives and so on, so much better than the ironically named Mothers Pride.

Brown bread can be quite misleading. Often it means white bread with added caramel, or some other additive that gives it colour. If you want to make a healthier choice you need to buy bread that is wholemeal not simply brown, and you will taste and see the difference.

Whilst processed sliced white bread lasts a comparatively long time, real bread needs to be looked after to ensure it lasts a good couple of days. When keeping bread it mustn't be tightly sealed, but kept in a container with enough space for air to circulate, as bread gives off moisture and if it isn't allowed to 'breathe', mould will grow very quickly. To have a ready supply of real bread, loaves can be frozen if well wrapped, but take it out of its wrapper as quickly as possible to thaw it at room temperature.

nwfinefoodawards 2007

Best HOT
PUDDING
OR DESSERT

Plumgarths Farmshop
Sticky Toffee Pudding

To qualify puddings or desserts must use regional produce using free range eggs if applicable. It must not contain any hydrogenated fat, artificial colourings or flavourings. This is always a hotly contested category, and for the first time Plumgarths Farmshop won the award with their own Sticky Toffee Pudding. Judges commented that it was everything a pudding should be – not too sweet or cloying, hugely satisfying and a little bit wicked!

Paul Harrison
Plumgarths Farmshop, Lakeland Food Park, Crook Road, Kendal, Cumbria LA8 8QJ
phone 01539 736300
www.plumgarths.co.uk

Availability: Farm shop on-site or mail order by phone.

Angela's Pantry

Angela Thompson
90 Turks Road, Radcliffe,
Greater Manchester M26 4QB
phone 0161 723 0615
www.angelaspantry.com

Availability: Available from Angela's permanent stall at Botany Bay, Chorley and at specialised food festivals and farmers' markets. Also available online from www.northernharvest.co.uk

Description: Specialist baker famed for producing unique themed celebration cakes, gingerbread houses and churches, mediaeval gingerbread and edible flower collections. All ingredients are free range/organic where possible, and free from all artificial colours, flavourings and preservatives. A gluten and dairy free range is also available.

Cartmel Sticky Toffee Pudding Co Ltd

Howard & Jean Johns
The Bakery, Moor Lane,
Flookburgh, Grange-over-Sands,
Cumbria LA11 7LS
phone 01539 558300
email
nicepeople@stickytoffeepudding.co.uk
www.stickytoffeepudding.co.uk

Availability: Available at fine food outlets throughout the UK and from the Cartmel Village Shop.

Description: Manufacturers of the award winning famous Cartmel Sticky Toffee Pudding, available from their Cartmel shop and across the UK. Made to a traditional Lakeland recipe using only the finest ingredients.

Cheshire Chocolates

Amanda & David Torkington
22 Brookside Lane, High Lane,
Stockport, Cheshire SK6 8HL
phone 01663 763309
email
amanda@cheshirechocolates.co.uk
www.cheshirechocolates.co.uk

Availability: Available from fine food retailers throughout Cheshire and the North West and online from their website.

Description: Every chocolate is individually hand made using only the finest Belgium couverture and locally sourced ingredients to unique recipes. They are presented in fine quality packaging suitable for any occasion. Winner of North West Producer of the Year 2005 for Best Chocolate.

Classic Desserts Ltd

Alan Armstrong
Unit 19-21,
Blencathra Business Centre,
Threlkeld, Cumbria CA12 4TR
phone 01768 779043
email alan@classicdesserts.co.uk
www.classicdesserts.co.uk

Availability: Available to the trade only.

Description: Classic Desserts Ltd make and supply a range of high quality handmade desserts and puddings to the wholesale trade. A new range of delicious puddings has recently been launched.

nwfinefoodawards 2007

The Cultured Bean
Bitter Chocolate Torte

This category included sweet or fruit pastries.
Judges looked for texture, taste and visual
appearance with pastry that is well cooked and
melts in the mouth. The contents of the pastry
needed to work well with the filling, juice or integral
sauces, which should be appropriate in amount
and texture. When Sharon Canavan and her
daughter Leanne Entwistle opened The Cultured
Bean in 2004, their aim was to serve the finest
quality dessert and patisserie menu, and refuse to
pay homage to the fast food industry. The judges
feel they have more than achieved their ambition.
They were full of praise for the bitter choloate torte
describing it as "silky, chocolate heaven" and
"outstanding taste and quality of chocolate".

Sharon Canavan
The Cultured Bean, 9a Bridge Street, Ramsbottom,
Lancashire BL0 9AB
phone 01706 825232

Availability: Available in their café in Ramsbottom.

Best
SWEET
PASTRY

Corby Chocolates

Ruth Samuels
Firwood Cottage, Mottram Road,
Alderley Edge, Cheshire SK9 7DW
phone 01625 865671
www.corbychocolates.co.uk

Availability: Available by mail
order, please visit the website
for further details.

Description: Delicious, mouth-
watering luxury handmade
chocolate truffles are packaged
for high quality retail outlets, and
can be supplied in hand-
decorated boxes for weddings,
special occasions and corporate
events. Producer of the Year 2004
"Award of Excellence" for
their White Chocolate
Champagne Truffle.

Country Fare

Dianne Halliday
Dalefoot Farm,
Mallerstang, Kirkby Stephen,
Cumbria CA17 4JT
phone 01768 372519
www.country-fare.co.uk

Availability: Available by mail
order on their website (also see
full list of stockists), and at Farmers'
Markets and food retailers
across Cumbria.

Description: Country Fare is an
award winning family business
producing quality hand made
cakes, biscuits and puddings
using the finest local ingredients.
Traditional, tried and tested
recipes are made on a working
farm by farmers' wives in a
converted 17th Century barn.
Country Fare are winners of
many Great Taste awards.

Country Puddings

Lynne Mallinson
Lodge Farm, Dacre, Penrith,
Cumbria CA11 0HH
phone 017684 86675
email
info@countrypuddings.co.uk
www.countrypuddings.co.uk

Availability: Available from delicatessens, farm shops, food halls and restaurants across the UK and online through their website.

Description: Lynne Mallinson produces her delicious puddings and sauces from a purpose built kitchen in a converted barn at Lodge Farm, the family home and a working dairy farm. It is situated in the Lakeland village of Dacre nestling in a valley two miles from Lake Ullswater.

De La Tierra

Janet Handley
41 Whitfield Cross,
Glossop, Stockport,
Greater Manchester SK13 8NW
phone 01457 868917
email
janet@delatierrachocolates.co.uk
www.delatierrachocolates.co.uk

Availability: Available at food events and farmers' markets across the region and by mail order through their website.

Description: Handmade chocolates using the finest ingredients (sourced locally wherever possible) infused with flowers, herbs and spices. Their single origin bean chocolate is created from cocoa beans from small producers in some of the best cocoa regions in the world.

Duerden's Confectionery

Trevor & Niels Duerden
Unit 8, Oxford Mill, Holgate Street,
Harle Syke, Burnley,
Lancashire BB10 2HQ
phone 01282 613747

Availability: Available from farmers' and fine foods markets and Asda stores in Manchester and the surrounding area. Please call for further details.

Description: Established in 1922 by the grandparents of the present owner, Duerden's produce high quality fudges and toffee using original family recipes, some of which date back to the middle 1800's.

Farmhouse Biscuits Ltd

Philip McIvor and Tony Birbeck
Mill Brook Street, Nelson,
Lancashire BB9 9PX
phone 01282 613520
email mcivor@farmhouse-biscuits.co.uk
www.farmhouse-biscuits.co.uk

Availability: Available nationally through a network of wholesalers, caterers, retail outlets and their own factory shop. Ring for further details.

Description: Manufacturers of the finest traditional hand baked biscuits with over 200 different original recipes which are all attractively packaged. Highly decorated and collectable gift tins available with products for every occasion. Other services include own label, health biscuits for coeliacs, high fibre, low sugar, high protein, organic, etc.

Farmhouse Fare Ltd

Helen Colley
Anderson House,
Lincoln Way, Salthill, Clitheroe,
Lancashire BB7 1QL
phone 01200 453110
email puds@farmhousefare.co.uk
www.farmhousefare.co.uk

Availability: Widely available from most major supermarkets.

Description: Hand crafted preservative-free nursery style puddings, made in rural Lancashire. Winners of dozens of awards, Farmhouse Fare remain true to the pursuit of great taste combined with the highest quality.

Hazelmere Cafe and Bakery

Ian & Dorothy Stubley
1 & 2 Yewbarrow Terrace,
Grange-over-Sands,
Cumbria LA11 6ED
phone 01539 532972

Availability: Available daily from the café at Grange-over-Sands.

Description: Traditional bakers and confectioners of high quality products working to both local and original recipes and using only the best ingredients. All ingredients are sourced locally where possible.
An extensive range of home made preserves, chutneys and jams is also available.

nwfinefoodawards 2007

Best BISCUIT

Brunswick Deli
Caramel Shortcake

To qualify biscuits must use regional produce where possible and not contain any hydrogenated fat, artificial colourings or flavourings. Judges looked for texture, taste and visual appearance with a biscuit that had a good crunch, was well cooked and melted in the mouth. Judges loved the Caramel Shortcake which had just enough sweetness, with a balance of soft caramel and biscuity crunch. This busy deli in Penrith specialises in homemade meals, puddings, biscuits and freshly prepared baguettes. With two NW Fine Food Awards this year, Susan obviously knows how to win over the judges.

Susan Bell
Brunswick Deli, 9 Brunswick Road, Penrith, Cumbria CA11 7LU
phone 01768 210500

Availability: Available in the deli in Penrith.

John Pimblett & Sons Ltd

Lin Pimblett
College Bakery, College Street,
St Helens, Merseyside WA10 1TP
phone 01744 455500
email info@pimbletts.co.uk
www.pimbletts.co.uk

Availability: Available by mail
order, or from one of their shops
in Lancashire and Merseyside.
Ring for further details.

Description: A refreshing blend of
craftsmanship baking, combined
with a strong modern approach.
Innovative leaders as design
consultants of wedding cakes
and confections. Awards in
abundance, not only for
outstanding, consistent quality
and presentation of goods,
but also national recognition
for training in customer care.

Munx Lakeland Bakery

Aidan Monks and Sara Hall
9-11 Mill Yard, Staveley, Kendal,
Cumbria LA8 9LR
phone 01539 822102

Availability: Available from the
bakery and from food outlets
throughout Cumbria and North
Lancashire. Please call for
further details.

Description: Munx Lakeland
Bakery is an independent baker,
producing traditional bread,
speciality bread and patisserie
using the finest ingredients and
craftsmanship. This, combined
with their passion for the product
creates bread with the most
amazing texture, aroma, and
of course, taste.

M Ray Ltd

Michele Ray
39-45 High Street, Prescot,
Merseyside L34 6HF
phone 0151 426 6148
www.mrays.com

Availability: All products available from the shop in Prescot. M Rays Puddings are also available from fine food outlets throughout the UK.

Description: Established in 1924, this award winning high class baker supplies a full range of bakery products to both the retail and wholesale trades.
Also creators of 'Mrs Rays Pudding Company' manufacturers of very special Christmas puddings and mince pies.

Mary's Homemade Cakes

Mary Walton
3 Weatherstones Mews,
Hanns Hall Road, Willaston,
South Wirral, Cheshire CH64 7TF
phone 0151 336 4720
www.maryscakes.co.uk

Availability: Available at farmers' markets throughout Merseyside, please call for further details.

Description: Baker of quality handmade fruit cakes, gourmet flapjacks, scones, muffins and Christmas puddings, using the best ingredients, sourced locally wherever possible.

Notes on chocolate

Chocolate is the only food that melts at body temperature. This alone gives you the feeling that somehow it understands us and our bodies, and the hit it gives you can only ever cheer you up.

When it goes into your mouth it melts and spreads over your tongue releasing it's held in sweetness. It's when it's just melted that all the flavours burst. Well made chocolate should be slightly bitter as well as sweet, a touch of butter, vanilla and a little sugar. Bad chocolate has a low cocoa solid content and will have a less rich flavour, so that more sugar needs to be added. Such products are overly sweet, can also be over roasted and contain unnecessary artificial ingredients. It gives a sugar hit and not a chocolate hit – not the same thing at all.

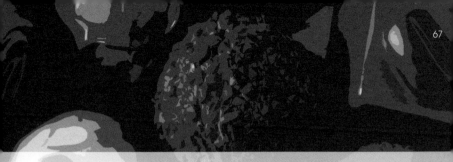

Chocolate doesn't necessarily need to be refrigerated, and is fine in naturally cold temperatures or up to around 20°C. It is more important to keep it at a constant temperature. Like wine and cheese, it needs to be slowly brought up to room temperature just before eating. That way you can rely on it to melt in your mouth and explode with reassuring natural sweetness at exactly the right time in your mouth.

If you want to buy a really good bar of chocolate look for those either with a high cocoa solid content, or even better with cocoa butter, and with vanilla, not vanillin. Plain dark chocolate should have a shininess that shows it's been cooked at the right temperature for the right amount of time, a balance of sweetness and bitterness and creamy cocoa-butter finish. The smooth texture should linger in your mouth and be invigoratingly bitter to begin with, but sweet and slightly fatty in the finish. Draw the curtains, sit on the settee and watch a comfortingly familiar movie, and make sure to eat it all yourself, this is not a time for friends or family!

nwfinefood awards 2007

Best
CHOCOLATE

Sarjeants Confectionery
Milk Chocolate Caramel Bar

To qualify chocolate must use regional produce where possible including local milk and cream and not contain any hydrogenated fat, artificial colourings or flavourings. Judges looked for well made chocolate with a touch of butter, vanilla and a little sugar, but not overly sweet. Sarjeants Confectionery is a chocolate manufacturer producing high quality handmade chocolate, including continental style truffles with over 30 flavours including Baileys, Amaretto and Whisky. Judges described their Milk Chocolate Caramel Bar as "rich caramel, simple and silky smooth".

Tom Lang
Sarjeants Confectionery, 28 Birkenhead Road, Hoylake, Wirral, Merseyside CH47 3BW
phone 0151 632 2399
www.sarjeants.co.uk

Availability: Available online from their website and from their Wirral shop.

Oakroyd Bakery

Emma Craven
17 Station Road, High Bentham,
North Yorkshire LA2 7LH
phone 01524 263353
www.oakroydbakery.co.uk

Availability: Available at high quality stores, farm shops, tourist attractions, and delicatessens, including Booths, The Country Harvest Farm Shop and Dobbies Garden Centre.

Description: A craft bakery making speciality breads, based on the edge of the Yorkshire Dales, making products by hand to traditional recipes. Winner of 4 Great Taste Awards including Gold for their Sticky Toffee Pudding.

Route Ginger

Sue Henshaw and Suzanne Bower
53 Clarendon Road, Sale,
Cheshire M33 2DY
phone 0161 973 7031

Availability: Available at farmers' markets and by mail order.

Description: Seasonal homegrown and locally grown produce in this bakery making home made cakes, traditional puddings, pies, tarts and also a large selection of jams, curds, conserves, honey, chutneys, pickles and relishes. Specialty mince pies, cakes and Christmas puddings.

Sarjeants Confectionery

Tom Lang
28 Birkenhead Road, Hoylake,
Wirral, Merseyside CH47 3BW
phone 0151 632 2399
email tom@sarjeants.co.uk
www.sarjeants.co.uk

Availability: Available online from their website, and from their Wirral shop.

Description: Sarjeants Confectionery is a chocolate manufacturer, producing high quality handmade chocolate, including continental style truffles, crèmes and novelties. Over 30 flavours including Baileys, Amaretto and Whisky truffles.

Sugarcube

Jameelah Keane
26 Langthorne Street,
Levenshulme, Manchester,
Greater Manchester M19 2GR
phone 0161 442 3729

Availability: Available from fine food markets and events across the North West, please call for more information.

Description: Sweets and confectionery from a bygone era, sold in cube-shaped boxes and hampers, hand finished with ribbon to create the perfect gift. With two different, yet equally tempting ranges, based around the concepts of 'Retro' and 'Nostalgia'.

nwfinefoodawards
2007

Le Chocolatier
Cheshire Cream Fudge

To qualify fudge must use regional produce where possible and not contain any hydrogenated fat, artificial colourings or flavourings. Judges looked for a rich taste where the sweetness wasn't too overpowering. Michael Levy is a Master Chocolate Maker and founded Le Chocolatier in his kitchen in 1993. They supply many Michelin Starred restaurants around the UK, and also sell high quality ingredients for chocolate and fudge making. Judges thought this fudge had a "lovely appearance and nice texture".

Michael Levy
Le Chocolatier, 8 Barrowmore Estate, Great Barrow, Chester CH3 7JA
phone 01289 741010

Availability: In high class restaurants and at food events and food shows in the North West.

Best
FUDGE

Susan's Farmhouse Fudge

Susan & Andrew Rigg
Gregson's Farm, Samlesbury,
Preston, Lancashire PR5 0UH
phone 01772 877468

Availability: Available from
farmers' markets - please call
for further details.

Description: A family based
business, that produce quality
homemade fudge, toffee,
hand-made chocolate animals
and truffles. Made with no
artificial preservatives they are,
undoubtedly, "a taste of the
good old days".

Sweet Home Ambleside

Gaynor Withers
Briardale, Millans Park, Ambleside,
Cumbria LA22 9AG
phone 01539 434203
www.sweethomeambleside.co.uk

Availability: Available from fine
food outlets and farmers' markets
across Cumbria and the North
West - please call for
further details.

Description: Delicious hand
made puddings for party
people. Currently products
include a Date and Sticky Toffee
Pudding, Chocolate and
Damson Pudding, Chocolate and
Cherry Pudding and Cranberry
and Orange Pudding.

Taylors Classics Ltd

Paul Taylor and Stephen Armstrong
Unit 1, Borders Business Park,
Longtown, Carlisle,
Cumbria CA6 5TD
phone 01228 792923
email sales@taylorsclassics.co.uk
www.taylorsclassics.co.uk

Availability: Available by mail order, and online via the website. Also from Harvey Nichols Foodmarket, and other fine food outlets throughout the region.

Description: Taylors Classics' range of desserts include Bread and Butter Pudding, Sticky Toffee Pudding and the gluten free Chocolate Slab, all of which are individually hand made with only the finest ingredients by chef Paul Taylor.

Ultimate Plum Pudding Company

Bernice Humphreys
10 Beezon Estate, Kendal,
Cumbria LA9 6BW
phone 01539 733329
email
sales@ultimateplumpudding.co.uk
www.ultimateplumpudding.co.uk

Availability: Widely available from outlets across the UK, including Booths and Lakeland Ltd.

Description: Producer of the "Gold" Great Taste Award winning Christmas puddings. Puddings supplied for retail, catering, private label and packaged for company gifts. Other products available include Triple Ginger Pudding, Chocolate Pudding and Brandy Butter.

nwfinefoodawards
2007

Best CAKE

Brunswick Deli
Chocolate Brownie

To qualify, cakes must use regional produce where possible and not contain any hydrogenated fat, artificial colourings or flavourings. Judges looked for texture, taste and visual appearance. Judges were bowled over by these Chocolate Brownies. They described them as having a "lovely dense texture" and one judge even went so far as to say this made "the perfect dessert", whilst another simply described them as "excellent". This busy deli in Penrith specialises in homemade meals, puddings, cakes, biscuits and freshly prepared baguettes. With two NW Fine Food Awards this year, Susan obviously knows how to win over the judges.

Susan Bell
Brunswick Deli, 9 Brunswick Road, Penrith, Cumbria CA11 7LU
phone 01768 210500

Availability: Available in the deli in Penrith.

Village Bakery (Melmerby) Ltd

Lindsay Williams
Melmerby, Penrith,
Cumbria CA10 1HE
phone 01768 881811
www.village-bakery.com

Availability: Widely available throughout the UK, outlet search function available on their website.

Description: Award-winning specialist bakery producing a wide variety of organic breads, cakes and biscuits baked in wood-fired ovens. All products are certified organic by the Soil Association. The bakery also runs very popular hands-on 'Bread Matters' bread making courses.

William Santus & Co Ltd

John Winnard and Anita Taulty
The Toffee Works, Dorning Street,
Wigan, Lancashire WN1 1HE
phone 01942 243464
email unclejoe@uncle-joes.com
www.uncle-joes.com

Availability: Available from Uncle Joe's Emporium on Crompton Street in Wigan and from Asda, Tesco, Morrisons, Lakeland Ltd, Harvey Nichols and House of Bruar.

Description: Traditional manufacturers of high quality confectionery including the traditional, and world famous, Uncle Joe's Mintballs. Uncle Joe's are 100% natural, containing no artificial colours or additives, they are GM free, gluten free and are suitable for vegans. The recipe has been passed down generations and still remains a closely guarded secret.

Meat

Fresh meat, poultry and game

Prepared fresh meats

Speciality meat

Bacon

Air dried meat

Cooked and smoked meats

Continental style meats

Sausages

Black pudding

nwfinefoodawards 2007

Best FRESH MEAT and **Best FARMED POULTRY OR GAME**

Johnson & Swarbrick
Corn Fed Goosnargh Duck

The category includes fresh beef, lamb, goat, pork, farmed poultry and game, prepared meats and speciality meats. The judges felt the meat category was particularly strong this year, with the amount of very high quality beef a real asset to the North West. However it is the Corn Fed Goosnargh Duck which won the overall category. Johnson & Swarbrick are producers of Goosnargh Duckling and Corn Fed Chickens, and are a well known quality supplier to restaurateurs including Gordon Ramsay, Paul Heathcote, Marco Pierre White and Nigel Haworth. Judges described this product as having "excellent, dense flesh" and "moist, robust and full of flavour".

Reg Johnson
Johnson & Swarbrick, Swainson House Farm, Goosnargh Lane, Goosnargh, Preston, Lancashire PR3 2JU.
phone 01772 865251
www.jandsgoosnargh.co.uk

Availability: Wholesale to the trade and at the Farm in Goosnargh, visit the website for details.

Notes on charcuterie

For thousands of years pigs have been kept by man, and prized for their ability to thrive where other animals starved, and the fact that nearly the whole of its body is edible.

Hams from the legs can be salted and air-dried or smoked, other parts minced to be preserved in patés. Then of course, there is bacon, sausages, salamis, pancetta, or you could eat its liver, trotters, ears, or salt-dry its cheeks eaten as chaps, or the head made into brawn. Even the blood, thickened with oatmeal or barley can be used to make black pudding.

These cured, dried and salted pork products are generally known as charcuterie. Well preserved hams are relatively dry and much denser than the mass produced alternative which is flabby, lightweight and slimy. Often these will have an artificially high water content, have been soaked in brine with a dubious pink colour, and even one slice could be reconstituted from pigs from two or three different countries, none of which will be in the UK, and may come from any part of the pig not just the leg muscle.

Good ham uses meat from a pig that is at least seven months old, so that the flavour has time to mature. Some are so good you can even detect the food the pig has been fed. My favourite is dry cure ham which involves rubbing the pork with salt and saltpetre and sometimes sugar and spice, leaving it for a few weeks, washing and drying it, then hanging it to mature for a month or two. After that it could be smoked or cooked. By contrast fast-track hams, produced on a large commercial scale, tend to use pigs that are as young as four or five months old, that are injected with brine, often containing artificial flavours, preservatives and gelling agents to keep the water in and boost the weight. Such hams can be ready to cook within two days.

nwfinefoodawards 2007

Best BEEF

The Worrall House Farm Larder
Home Produced Sirloin Steak

To qualify the animal must have been raised in the region for a minimum of 6 months or half its life, whichever is the shorter, and must have been slaughtered and prepared in the region. The beef category was simply stunning with the quality and number of entries a real delight. However, this Home Produced Sirloin Steak was a clear winner with all the judges. Comments included "beautiful flavour, melting and moist", "fantastic, a clear winner" and "wow". The Worrall House Farm Larder is an established farm shop selling their own grass fed Aberdeen Angus beef, as well as home cured bacon, gammon and a large variety of handmade sausages, along with local pork, lamb, cornfed and free range chickens.
If you're in the area go there now and buy this steak it's marvellous.

Diane Edwards
Worrall House Farm, Flatmans Lane, Downholland, Nr Ormskirk, Lancashire L39 7HW.
phone 0151 527 1210
www.farmerteds.com

Availability: Retail farmshop.

Albert's

Paul Aspinall
Unit E, Meat and Fish Hall,
The Famous Bury Market,
Murray Road, Bury,
Lancashire BL9 0BJ
phone 0161 761 4488
email orders@albertsdirect.co.uk
www.albertsdirect.co.uk

Availability: Available at
Bury Market.

Description: Suppliers of the very
finest British meat. They also offer
award winning sausages and
traditional dry cured bacon.
All their meat is extra matured to
bring out the flavour and assure
tenderness. They are suppliers
to discerning restaurants, pubs
and hotels.

Alpe's The Butchers Ltd

George Alpe
14 Shawbridge Street, Clitheroe,
Lancashire BB7 1LZ
phone 01200 424519

Availability: Shop on site.

Description: Traditional butchers
shop which pays attention to
detail. They are Gold Award
winners for sausages and their
beef is grass fed Heifer beef,
hung for twenty one days to
assure quality. They have both deli
and hot counters selling barbeque
meats and fresh made hot and
cold sandwiches and pies.
All products are locally sourced.
Member of the Guild of Q Butchers.

Althams Catering Butchers

David Keating
Northgate, White Lund Ind Estate,
Morecambe, Lancashire LA3 3AY
phone 01524 33433
email sales@j-c-althams.com
www.j-c-althams.com

Availability: Trade sales only.

Description: Althams Catering
Butchers are probably one of
the largest independent family
run businesses in the country
with "hands on" directors.
Their company is committed
to customer care and are an
EC licensed factory offering
specialist meat, poultry and
charcuterie using local, national
and international products all
with total traceability.

Andrews Continental Delicacies

Christopher Unsworth
Units 2-4 Muslin Street, Salford,
Greater Manchester M5 4NF
phone 0161 745 8449

Availability: Manchester Fine
Food Markets and to the trade.

Description: Producer of
continental sausages using
authentic recipes including
chorizo, frankfurters and kabanos,
but using locally sourced meat
and ingredients. Also hams and
gammon, turkey and lamb.

nwfinefoodawards
2007

JW Mettrick & Son Ltd
Herdwick Lamb Chop

Best LAMB
OR GOAT

To qualify the animal must have been raised in the region for a minimum of 6 months or half its life, whichever is the shorter. The lamb or goat must also have been slaughtered and prepared in the region. The judges were really impressed by the Herswick Lamb Chops' depth of taste. John Mettrick is a fifth generation family butcher well known for very high quality meat sourced from local farms withn a 10 mile radius and processed in their own abattoir. They won BBC 4's Food and Farming Awards Best Local Food Retailer for 2005/2006, and rightly deserved this award too. Judges described the chops as "tender and tasty with a long follow through".

John Mettrick
JW Mettrick & Son Limited, 20/22 High Street West, Glossop, Stockport, Greater Manchester SK13 8BH
phone 01457 852239
www.highpeaklamb.co.uk

Availability: Shop online and wholesale to the trade.

Baileys Turkeys

Michael Bailey
Dairy House Farm,
Chester Road, Tabley, Knutsford,
Cheshire WA16 0PN.
phone 01565 632174
email sales@baileysturkeys.co.uk
www.baileysturkeys.co.uk

Availability: Farm shop and
wholesale to the trade.

Description: Producers and
processors of fresh turkeys
and turkey meat products.
Specialising in the preparation
of turkey meat to individual
customer requirements available
at the farm shop or to the trade.

Bennetts Quality Meats Ltd

Martyn Bennett
28 Princess Parade, Bury,
Lancashire BL9 0QL
phone 0161 761 1501

Availability: Shop on site.

Description: Third generation
family butchers sourcing only
the finest home produced lamb,
pork, chicken and matured beef.
Traditional butchery alongside
many national award winning
products, home made award
winning sausages and dry cured
bacon. Their popular hot counter
stocks hot roast meats, alongside
home made chilli, curry, potato
pie and cottage pie. Member of
the Guild of Q Butchers.

Border County Foods

Jackie Davies
The Old Vicarage,
Crosby on Eden, Carlisle,
Cumbria CA6 4QZ
phone 01228 573500
email jhd@cumberland-sausage.net
www.cumberland-sausage.net

Availability: Farmers' Markets,
mail order and online.

Description: Fantastic rare breed
free range pork products, gluten
free Cumberland sausage,
cured pork, black pudding and
Cumberland dux. Venison, rabbit,
wild wood pigeon and all other
in-season game.

Bowland Outdoor Reared Pork

Tony Holland
Bradshaw Barn,
Craggs Farm, Lowgill, Tatham,
Lancashire LA2 8RB
phone 01524 263031

Availability: Farmers' Markets in
the Fylde area. Their website gives
further information.

Description: High quality pork
products from home-reared pigs
reared in the Forest of Bowland.
Their product range includes dry
cured bacon and gammon,
Bowland pork sausages,
burgers and fresh pork joints.
Also available, Hog Roast and
catering BBQ for private parties,
functions and events.

nwfinefoodawards 2007

Best PORK

Udale Speciality Foods
Gloucester Old Spot Pork Loin Steak

To qualify the animal must have been raised in the region for a minimum of 6 months or half its life, whichever is the shorter. The pig must also have been slaughtered and prepared in the region. The judges were unanimous in their praise for the Gloucester Old Spot Pork Loin Steak, with comments such as "lovely texture", "super piece of meat" and "oustanding". Probably the best comment came from David Gale of Selfridges who simply said "great bit of pig". Udale Speciality Foods are a long established and traditionally run family business supplying local fresh meat, poultry, game and regional fine foods to premier hotels and restaurants throughout the Lake District, North Lancashire and surrounding areas.

Ian & Neil Udale
Udale Speciality Foods, Schola Green Lane, Morecambe, Lancashire LA4 5QT
phone 01524 411611
www.udale.com

Availability: Wholesale to the trade.

Brendan Anderton Butchers Ltd

Austin Anderton
19-21 Derby Road, Longridge,
Preston, Lancashire PR3 3JT
phone 01772 783321

Availability: Shop on site.

Description: Traditional family butchers and high class catering supplier, using locally sourced high quality meats. Renowned not only for their fresh meat but also their cooked meat counter. Member of the Guild of Q Butchers.

Brough Butchers Ainsdale

Stephen Ashton
581 Liverpool Road, Ainsdale,
Southport, Merseyside PR8 3LU
phone 01704 574069
email stephen@broughs.com
www.broughs.com

Availability: Shop on site.

Description: Brough Butchers' reputation for best practice in the procurement and supply of fresh meat products ensures consistent results for their customers. They have an extensive range of creative meat products, including marinades to provide tasty meal options. The full compliment of their award winning sausage and bacon products are also available.

Brough Butchers Birkdale

David Allen
20 Liverpool Road, Birkdale,
Southport, Merseyside PR8 4AY
phone 01704 567073
email dave@broughs.com
www.broughs.com

Availability: Shop on site.

Description: The Birkdale
establishment is an excellent
example of the 'traditional'
butchers shop featuring an original
'pay office' and the Victorian tiled
walls. Many of the products on
offer are award winning, they are
innovative and delicious. Regional
Winners of Best Sausage 2004.

Brough Butchers Formby

Robert Powell
36B Chapel Lane, Formby,
Merseyside L37 4DU
phone 01704 872075
email rob@broughs.com
www.broughs.com

Availability: Shop on site.

Description: The Formby shop
is the first of the Brough Butchers
group to offer customers a hot
food option, the chef prepares
the hot food and revises the
innovative and creative menu
each day. Award winning sausage
and a delicious range of freshly
prepared cooked meats.

Brough Butchers Ormskirk

Mark Shepherd
10 Burscough Street, Ormskirk,
Lancashire L39 2ER
phone 01695 570600
email mark@broughs.com
www.broughs.com

Availability: Shop on site.

Description: Their kitchen ready range is mouth watering and comes with advice on cooking and serving suggestions from the well informed staff. Award winning sausages, prize winning bacon and a full range of freshly prepared cooked meats.

Callaghan G & Son

Howard & Gordon Callaghan
8 Central Square, Maghull,
Liverpool, Merseyside L31 0AE
phone 0151 526 9345

Availability: Shop on site.

Description: Established in 1970 Callaghan's are traditional butchers offering British lambs and Scotch beef. They specialise in marinated and ready made meats. They make their own sausages and cooked meats and also have a hot sandwich counter - have won Best Butcher 1993 and 1996. Member of the Guild of Q Butchers.

NW Fine Food and The Guild of Q Butchers

Members of the Guild of Q Butchers are recognised as Britain's finest independent butchers. Q butchers are the only meat retailers who voluntarily submit to regular Q audits to rigorous standards of technical excellence.

Members promote traditional butchery craft skills and are committed to supporting the British farming industry with home produced beef, lamb, pork, game and poultry. They are independently audited to "above the norm" standards of quality and hygiene by the European Food Safety Inspection Service. Membership is one of the meat industry's highest endorsements of excellence, and NW Fine Food is proud to have a number of Guild of Q Butchers as our members too:

Alpe's The Butchers Ltd
Bennetts Quality Meats Ltd
Brendan Anderton Butchers Ltd
Callaghan G & Son
Cheerbrook Quality Farm Food Ltd
Cranstons Ltd
David Wearden Quality Fresh Foods
FB Taylor & Son Ltd
Frasers Butchers Ltd
H Clewlow Butchers
Higginsons Ltd
JT Vernon Ltd
JW Mettrick & Son Ltd
Steadmans
The Scotch Beef Shop
WH Frost (Butchers) Ltd

Capra Products

Gillian McManoman
Marimar, Cumeragh Lane,
Whittingham, Preston,
Lancashire PR3 2AN.
phone 01772 784881
www.capraproducts.co.uk

Availability: For availability,
telephone for further details.

Description: Famous quality
goats meat producer established
over twenty years. They offer meat,
sausage and a great range of
artisan cheeses.

The Chadwick Family Emporium of Fine Foods

Paul Chadwick
& Jeanette Chadwick
Wellington Place,
51 High Street, Standish, Wigan,
Lancashire WN6 0HD.
phone 01257 421137
www.noelchadwick.co.uk

Availability: Shop on site.

Description: Award winning
butchers, delicatessen, café
and restaurant, all under one roof.
One of a select band of butchers
that can truly claim traceability
through the slaughter process
right on to the plate.

Cheerbrook Quality Farm Foods Ltd

Andrew & Sarah Shufflebotham
Cheerbrook Farm,
Newcastle Road, Nantwich,
Cheshire CW5 7EL
phone 01270 666431
www.cheerbrook.co.uk

Availability: Shop on site.

Description: Award winning farm shop, food hall and butchery counter offering locally reared beef, pork and lamb, free range chicken and award winning sausages. Delicious range of ready meals, fine wines, cheese, local honey, fresh bread daily, homemade cakes, ice cream, jams and preserves. Member of the Guild of Q Butchers.

Gordon H Clark (Butchers Ltd)

Gordon & Gillian Clark
23 Great Dockray, Penrith,
Cumbria CA11 7DE
phone 01768 868689 (shop)

Availability: Shop on site.

Description: Continuing a family tradition since the early 1800's, Clarke's prepare quality fresh meats, locally sourced and cut to customers' requirements. Traditional cuts of beef, lamb, and pork, succulent steaks, freshly sliced bacon, home cooked meats, sausages and burgers including their renowned Cumberland sausage, all made on the premises.

H Clewlow Butchers

Charles Clewlow
and Adrian Spender
8 Pepper Street, Nantwich,
Cheshire CW5 5AB
phone 01270 625366
email sales@clewlows.co.uk
www.clewlows.co.uk

Availability: Shop on site.

Description: Traditional butchers selling beef, lamb and pork selected from local farms. Clewlow's sell many award winning products including pies, sausages, cooked meat and kitchen ready meals. Regional winner at the Great Taste Awards 2004 for Huntsman Pie. Member of the Guild of Q Butchers.

Cockers Farm Shop

Karen Allen and
Laurence & Barbara Catterall
Long Lane, Limbrick, Chorley,
Lancashire PR6 9EE
phone 01257 260743

Availability: Shop on site.

Description: Great farm shop selling organic and naturally produced meats and poultry, and a range of home made natural jams, preserves and ready meals. If you ask they will also make meals to take home to your own recipe.

Conder Green Farm Shop

James Lamb
Conder Green Farm,
Conder Green, Lancaster,
Lancashire LA2 0AN
phone 01524 752174
email
info@condergreenfarm.co.uk
www.condergreenfarm.co.uk

Availability: Farm shop and regular farmers' markets in the North West.

Description: Working farm selling home produced beef, pork and lamb. Also burgers and sausages made by hand from their own produce. Specialities include prize winning dry cured bacon and gammon.

Cranstons Ltd

Philip Cranston and John Cowen
Ullswater Road, Penrith,
Cumbria CA11 7EH
phone 01768 868680
email info@cranstons.net
www.cranstons.net

Availability: Own shops and to the trade.

Description: Cranstons specialise in high quality local produce available either from their own chain of shops or regional supermarkets, farm shops, delicatessens and caterers. A large and varied range of ready meals, sausages, pies, bacon and fresh meat are produced from their purpose built premises with distribution through their own transport. Member of the Guild of Q Butchers.

nwfinefoodawards
2007

Frasers Butchers
Stuffed Pork Fillet

To qualify the animal must have been raised in the region for a minimum of 6 months or half its life, whichever is the shorter, and must have been slaughtered and prepared in the region. Frasers Butchers are a high class family butchers specialising in Orkney Gold beef, Bronze turkeys and speciality sausages, but it is the Stuffed Pork Fillet which really impressed the judges. This comment pretty much summed up this wonderfully prepared piece of fresh meat, "loved it, an excellent combination of flavours and consistency".

Greg Hull
Frasers Butchers, 272 Rishton Lane, Great Lever, Bolton, Greater Manchester BL3 2EH
phone 01204 523278

Availability: Shop on site.

Best
PREPARED
FRESH MEAT

Cumbrian Fellbred Products Ltd

Joanne Gascoigne
Crooklands Road, Ackenthwaite,
Milnthorpe, Cumbria LA7 7LR
phone 01539 563232
email sales@fellbred.co.uk
www.fellbred.co.uk

Availability: Buy online, also wholesale butchers to the trade.

Description: Cumbrian Fellbred Products is a local catering butcher that sources and supplies Cumbrian meat from Cumbrian farms to hotels and restaurants. The company also supplies meat products direct to the public online under the Cumbrian Fellbred 'Direct' banner. All meat bearing the Fellbred name has been traditionally reared on Cumbrian farms.

Diggles Ltd

Colin Twiname
56 North Road, Lancaster,
Lancashire LA1 1LT
phone 01524 62060
email colin@diggles.co.uk
www.diggles.co.uk

Availability: Available wholesale to the trade.

Description: Manufacturers of traditional hams, natural beef, turkey and pork for the catering, wholesale, and retail trade. All products are available in varying pack sizes and can be sliced and labelled to each individual customer's requirements. Deliveries twice weekly throughout the North West.

Edge & Son

Callum Edge
61 New Chester Road, New Ferry,
Wirral, Merseyside CH62 1AB
phone 0151 645 3044
email
callum@traditionalmeat.com
www.traditionalmeat.com

Availability: Shop on site and wholesale to the trade.

Description: Established since 1844, specialising in rare breed and organic meats. All meat is traditionally butchered to the highest standard and left to hang for 2-4 weeks to ensure the finest taste and succulent texture. Edge & Son have a large selection of sausages, bacon and burgers and provide a butchery service for local producers.

Farmersharp

Andrew Sharp
Diamond Buildings,
Pennington Lane, Lindal-in-Furness,
Cumbria LA12 0LA
phone 01229 588299
www.farmersharp.co.uk

Availability: Online, at Borough Market and wholesale to the trade.

Description: Farmersharp is a supplier of Galloway Beef, Herdwick Lamb and Mutton, Pink Veal and a range of charcuterie products including Air Dried Herdwick Mutton Prosciutto, Herdwick Mutton Salami and Galloway Beef Bresaola. Their beef is hung for five weeks, their lamb for ten days and mutton for three weeks. Farmersharp supplies hotels, restaurants and delis.

Farmhouse Direct

David & Jacqueline Kitson
Long Ghyll Farms, Bleasdale Lane,
Bleasdale, Preston,
Lancashire PR3 1UZ
phone 01995 61799
email info@farmhousedirect.com
www.farmhousedirect.com

Availability: Shop on site, at NW
Fine Food Lovers Festivals and
farmers' markets, also mail
order online.

Description: Farmhouse Direct is
a small family run business selling
the finest quality meats direct from
their own farm. All animals are
naturally reared, producing safe,
healthy meats from traditional
British breeds with a quality and
flavour rarely seen. All processing
is done on the farm giving
maximum control from birth
to sale.

Foxhill Pedigree Pigs

Steven Wright
Foxhill Farm, Foxhill Lane, Liverpool,
Merseyside L26 4XG
phone 07795 246209
email steven@foxhillpigs.co.uk
www.foxhillpigs.co.uk

Availability: Farmers' markets in
Merseyside, and wholesale to
the trade.

Description: Foxhill Pedigree Pigs
make every effort to ensure their
animals lead a happy, healthy life.
Their farming methods ensure that
they rear their stock as naturally as
possible. This extensive method of
husbandry guarantees the highest
quality of life for their animals,
which in turn leads to high
quality meat.

nwfinefoodawards
2007

Tatton Park, Housekeeper's Store
Venison Sausage

Best
SPECIALITY
MEAT

To qualify the animal must have been raised in the region for a minimum of 6 months or half its life, whichever is the shorter, and must also have been slaughtered and prepared in the region. The judges loved this use of venison, describing its moistness and excellent taste. Tatton Park produce prime venison from the estate, including steaks, medallions or joints, premium hot smoked venison and quality potted venison, as well as this tasty Venison Sausage. The Housekeeper's Store in the Park sells all this estate reared produce and other products such as dry cured bacon, pork, rare breed or Park reared lamb.

Elizabeth Hough
Housekeeper's Store, Tatton Park, Knutsford, Cheshire WA16 6QN
phone 01625 534400
www.tattonpark.org.uk

Availability: Shop on site in the Park.

Frasers Butchers Ltd

Greg Hull
272 Rishton Lane,
Great Lever, Bolton,
Greater Manchester BL3 2EH
phone 01204 523278

Availability: Shop on site.

Description: High class family butchers specialising in Orkney Gold beef. Speciality sausage maker, home cured bacon, pork pies, cooked meats and Bronze turkeys. Member of the Guild of Q Butchers.

WH Frost (Butchers) Ltd

Lee Frost
12-14 Chorlton Place,
Wilbraham Road,
Chorlton, Manchester,
Greater Manchester M21 9AQ
phone 0161 881 8172

Availability: Shop on site and wholesale to the trade.

Description: A traditional family butchers owned, managed and run by the Frost family since 1910. Traditional methods combined with modern practices and family commitment to excellence make 'Frosts' unbeatable in quality, service, and reliability, from their thriving shop in Chorlton. They also supply many of the North West's leading hotels and restaurants. Member of the Guild of Q Butchers.

Gabbotts Farm Retail Ltd

Geoff Watson and Stephen Porter
Chaddock Lane, Astley, Tyldesley,
Greater Manchester M29 7JY
phone 01942 885320
email info@gabbottsfarm.co.uk
www.gabbottsfarm.co.uk

Availability: Shop on site.

Description: Gabbott's Farm are
established as a leading High
Street retailer with a range of
award winning sausages
produced using traditional
methods. They use prime cuts
of British pork and are hand linked
in natural casings at their modern
production unit in Astley.

The Great Tasting Meat Company

Andrew & Louise Jackson
Gate Farm,
Wettenhall Road, Poole, Nantwich,
Cheshire CW5 6AL
phone 01270 625781
email
andrew@greattastingmeat.co.uk
www.greattastingmeat.co.uk

Availability: Online and wholesale.

Description: Delicious award
winning meats come from grass-
fed, outdoor reared animals
whose welfare is paramount.
This ensures their progress from
farm to table is as stress free as
possible. The Great Tasting Meat
Co rear the slower-growing, rare
breeds such as Gloucester Old
Spot, Aberdeen Angus and
Suffolk Cross lambs for a well
developed flavour.

nwfinefoodawards
2007

Farmersharp
3 Month Air Dried Mutton

This category is another really strong one for the region. It includes bacon, air dried meat, cooked and smoked meats and continental style meats. To qualify meat must be produced in the North West using regional produce wherever possible, and the cooking process must be under the control, or supervision, of the producer. This 3 Month Air Dried Mutton really impressed the judges, with Farmersharp coming very close to being the Producer of the Year, with this stunning product in the Air Dried Meat category. Described as "beautiful, mature and with a strong flavour" by judges, their Galloway Beef Bresaola also came in for high praise. Farmersharp is a supplier of Galloway Beef, Herdwick Lamb and Mutton, Pink Veal and a range of charcuterie products including Air Dried Herdwick Mutton Prosciutto and Herdwick Mutton Salami. Their beef is hung for five weeks, their lamb for ten days and mutton for three weeks.

Andrew Sharp
Farmersharp, Diamond Buildings, Pennington Lane, Lindal-in-Furness, Cumbria LA12 0LA.
phone 01229 588299
www.farmersharp.co.uk

Availability: Online through their website, at Borough Market and wholesale to the trade.

Best CURED OR COOKED MEAT and **Best** AIR DRIED MEAT

Notes on bacon

A bacon sandwich has to be one of the finest breakfasts in the world. The sizzle in the pan, and the wafts of steam and heat that swirl around the kitchen, are enough to get the saliva going long before the hot and slightly crispy bacon hits the butter between the slices of bread.

The crispness, twang of salt, that slight sweetness, mixed with a little bit of natural meat spice also makes for a good combination with other smoother foods such as hot melted cheese or mashed potato. It's also great with scallops or with peppery salad leaves sprinkled with pine nuts that have been cooked in the bacon fat.

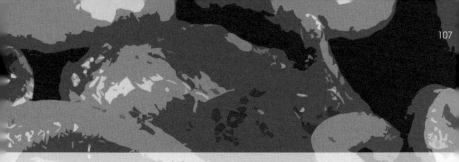

Much that can be said about poor ham products, apply to bacon. A good local butcher can sometimes be the only place where traditionally preserved bacon can be bought. This is dry-cured, made by rubbing salt into the raw flesh by hand, rather than soaking it in a bath full of brine, or injecting it with salt water through the pig's arteries. It takes longer, which makes it more expensive, but it is so tender, sweet and far tastier. The smell it gives off when cooking is worth the additional cost alone, and it's not really that much more expensive when you consider the weight is all meat, not added water.

Real bacon does not leave a white curd residue in the frying pan, and the rind goes crispy and golden so you can eat it like crackling, whereas brine injection or soaking leads to a horrid rind that is practically inedible, becoming tougher as it cooks. It can be smoked, but good unsmoked bacon, known as green bacon, has a more direct flavour, especially if it has been dry cured. It also allows the subtlety of the meat to shine through, where some smoked versions can mask the depth of the variety of flavours.

nwfinefoodawards 2007

Best BACON

The Cheshire Smokehouse
Sweet Black Back Bacon

To qualify bacon must be produced in the North West using regional produce wherever possible, and the cooking process must be under the control, or supervision, of the producer. This Sweet Black Back Bacon was absolutely delicious, cooking really well, with the judges describing it as "sweet, smoky and really tasty". This smokehouse in the heart of Cheshire produces a range of smoked meats, fish, game and nuts, all smoked on the premises, together with a wide range of accompaniments and complementary fine foods. There is an award winning café, a specialist patisserie and a renowned Fine Wine department. Along with this NW Fine Food Award, they are winners of the BBC 'Speciality Food Shop of the Year' 2002.

John and Darren Ward
The Cheshire Smokehouse, Vost Farm, Morley Green, Wilmslow, Cheshire SK9 5NU
phone 01625 548499
www.cheshiresmokehouse.co.uk

Availability: At the smokehouse shop near Wilmslow, with local deliveries to trade customers.

Hallsford Farm Produce

John Beattie and
Andrew & Helen Tomkins
Hallsford Farm Produce,
Hallsford, Hethersgill, Carlisle,
Cumbria CA6 6JD
phone 01228 577329
email info@hallsford.co.uk
www.hallsford.co.uk

Availability: NW Fine Food Lovers
Festivals, wholesale and online.

Description: Winners of the Fresh
Meat category in North West Fine
Foods Producer of the Year Awards
2003. Top quality marbled
Shorthorn beef, rare breed
Llanwenog lamb and Saddleback
pork from Cumbria. Other
seasonal produce such as
Herdwick lamb also available.

Higginsons Ltd

Stuart & Pauline Higginson
Keswick House, Main Street,
Grange-over-Sands,
Cumbria LA11 6AB
phone 01539 534367

Availability: Shop on site and
wholesale to the trade.

Description: Voted Britain's Best
Butchers, Higginsons produce an
extensive range of award winning
pies, sausages, home cured
bacon and hams. Traditional
and continental cuts of selected
Cumbrian produced beef, pork
and lamb. A speciality is Salt
Marsh Lamb reared locally.
Member of the Guild of Q Butchers.

The Hindquarter

Eric Danson and Charlotte Smith
1 Barton Square,
Knott End on Sea,
Poulton-Le-Fylde,
Lancashire FY6 0BN
phone 01253 810577

Availability: Shop on site.

Description: The Hindquarter is a high-class butchers shop providing quality meats, situated in the coastal village of Knott End. They promote full traceability and emphasis on reducing 'food miles', and are committed to excellent customer service. Their range includes homemade speciality sausage, home cured bacons and an extensive added value range.

Holly Tree Farm Shop

Karol Bailey
Holly Tree Farm,
Chester Road, Tabley, Knutsford,
Cheshire WA16 0EU
phone 01565 651835
www.hollytreefarmshop.co.uk

Availability: Farmshop on site and order via email, ring for details.

Description: Producers of fine quality lamb, turkeys, geese and ducks. In their shop there is a wide selection of handmade speciality sausages, pies, cakes and traditional dry cured bacon, all made on the premises. They are a Rare Breeds Accredited Butcher and a licensed meat cutting plant.

RS Ireland (The Real Lancashire Black Pudding Co.)

Andrew Holt
Unit 4, Waterside Industrial Estate,
Haslingden, Lancashire BB4 5EN
phone 01706 231029
www.rsireland.co.uk

Availability: Farmers' Markets and at NW Fine Food Lovers Festivals.

Description: This family run company, based in Rossendale, Lancashire are true specialists in their field. Producing the finest black and white puddings, they use only traditional methods and a recipe which dates back to 1879. Their attention to detail and quality has paid off, winning various awards throughout Europe.

Johnson & Swarbrick

Reg Johnson
Swainson House Farm,
Goosnargh Lane, Goosnargh,
Preston, Lancashire PR3 2JU
phone 01772 865251
www.jandsgoosnargh.co.uk

Availability: Wholesale to the trade and at the farm in Goosnargh, visit the website for details.

Description: Sole producers of Goosnargh Duckling and Corn Fed Chickens. Well known quality suppliers to restaurants and hotels in the region. A new range of smoked duckling and chicken are now available, and they can prepare goods to customer requirements.

Mansergh Hall Farm Shop

Jim Hadwin
Mansergh Hall, Kirkby Lonsdale,
Cumbria LA6 2EN
phone 01524 271397
email info@manserghhall.co.uk
www.manserghhall.co.uk

Availability: Shop on site and wholesale to the trade.

Description: Mansergh Hall lamb is highly acclaimed for its fantastic flavour and consistent quality, currently under conversion to fully organic status. Animal welfare is of major importance to them. They also produce beef, pork, sausages, bacon and gammon and stock local organic milk, chicken, eggs, fruit, vegetables and soup.

JW Mettrick & Son Ltd

John Mettrick
20/22 High Street West,
Glossop, Stockport,
Greater Manchester SK13 8BH
phone 01457 852239
email
john@mettricksbutchers.com
www.highpeaklamb.co.uk

Availability: Shop on site and wholesale to the trade.

Description: Fifth generation family butchers well known for very high quality meat sourced from local farms within a 10 mile radius and processed in their own abatoir. High Peak won Meat Trader Journal's Top Shop Award for Best Retail Butcher in England 2004/2005 and BBC 4's Food and Farming Awards Best Local Food Retailer 2005/2006. Member of the Guild of Q Butchers.

Pork Traders Oakwell Ltd

Nancy McKee
Holt Lane,
Netherby Industrial Estate,
Liverpool, Merseyside L27 2TB
phone 0151 457 7437
www.porktraders.co.uk

Availability: Supplied to
restaurants, retail, grocers
and butchers.

Description: Oakwell Brand is
a family run business producing
award winning black puddings
using the finest ingredients, sold
to trade customers. They are one
of the biggest producers in the UK
and have been established for
over 25 years.

Muffs of Bromborough

Steven Muff
5-7 Allport Lane, Bromborough,
Wirral, Merseyside CH62 7HH
phone 0151 334 2002
www.muffsonline.co.uk

Availability: Shop on site and
wholesale to the trade.

Description: Producers of the
finest sausages and meat
products using only ingredients
sourced in the North West.
Winners of countless accolades
over the years, including overall
best North West Product at the
Great Taste Awards 2003.

nwfinefood awards 2007

Foxhill Pedigree Pigs
Gammon Joint

To qualify meat must be produced in the North West using regional produce wherever possible, and the cooking process must be under the control, or supervision, of the producer. Judges loved this beautiful, traditional ham, with one going so far as to say "a couple of us wanted to smuggle this out of the judging room, to have with chips and mushy peas". Foxhill Pedigree Pigs make every effort to ensure their animals are reared as naturally as possible, and lead a happy, healthy life and this showed in the Gammon Joint's taste.

Steven Wright
Foxhill Pedigree Pigs, Foxhill Farm, Foxhill Lane, Liverpool, Merseyside L26 4XG
phone 07795 246209
www.foxhillpigs.co.uk

Availability: Farmers' markets in Merseyside, and wholesale to the trade.

Best
COOKED OR SMOKED MEAT

The Old Smokehouse and Brougham Hall Foods Ltd

Richard Muirhead
and Neil Harrison
Brougham Hall, Brougham, Penrith,
Cumbria CA10 2DE
phone 01768 867772
email sales@the-old-smokehouse.co.uk
www.the-old-smokehouse.co.uk

Availability: Shop on site and wholesale to the trade.

Description: The Old Smokehouse supply a range of smoked fish, poultry, game, meats, sausages and cheeses. Their products are from local sources wherever possible and are oak smoked without using artificial colourings, preserves or additives. In the shop at Brougham Hall they also make handmade truffles from the finest continental chocolate and the purest ingredients.

Parry Scragg Ltd

David Rawcliffe
25/33 Dalrymple Street,
Taylor Street Ind. Estate, Liverpool,
Merseyside L5 5HB
phone 0151 207 5867
www.parryscragg.co.uk

Availability: Wholesale to the trade.

Description: Manufacturers of traditional meat products since 1825. These include tripe, beef dripping, black pudding and savoury ducks. Now also a full range of burgers and sausages, supplied in individual retail packs or for catering and food service customers.

The Pie Mill

Jim & Amanda Hodge
Unit 16,
The Blencathra Business Centre,
Threlkeld Quarry, Keswick,
Cumbria CA12 4TR
phone 01768 779994
email info@piemill.co.uk
www.piemill.co.uk

Availability: Mail order online, at Booths and selected Farm shops.

Description: Piemill make a selection of hand made pies, using the freshest ingredients from local suppliers. The pastry is homemade and as short as possible to give the perfect texture. Their pies have plenty of meat, not just gravy, and they take great pride in the uniqueness of each hand finished pie. The Beef and Ale Pie was the winner of the National Pie of the Year competition 2005.

Pike End Farm

Martyn & Caroline Ryder
Pike End Farm,
Rishworth, Sowerby Bridge,
West Yorkshire HX6 4RG
phone 01422 823949
email info@pikeendfarm.net
www.pikeendfarm.net

Availability: Available on site at the farm and farmers' markets in Cheshire and Manchester. Also online box service and mail order.

Description: Pike End Farm raise their Dexter cattle to produce the finest beef. All their animals are grass fed with a little beet and barley in winter. They do not use medicines or concentrates, and after maturing for 21 days their beef is butchered and packed on the farm ready for cooking or freezing.

nwfinefoodawards
2007

Best
CONTINENTAL
STYLE MEAT

Andrews Continental Delicacies
Kabanos

To qualify meat must be produced in the North West using regional produce wherever possible, and the cooking process must be under the control, or supervision, of the producer.
The Kabanos were the judges favourite in this category being described as having a "good dense texture, with a good balance of meat and spice". Andrews Continental Delicacies produce continental sausages using authentic recipes including chorizo, frankfurters and kabanos, but using locally sourced meat and ingredients.

Christopher Unsworth
Andrews Continental Delicacies,
Units 2-4 Muslin Street, Salford,
Greater Manchester M5 4NF
phone 0161 745 8449

Availability: Manchester Fine Food Markets, North West food events and to the trade.

Plumgarths Farmshop

Steve Chambers and Paul Harrison
Lakeland Food Park, Crook Road,
Kendal, Cumbria LA8 8QJ
phone 01539 736300
email
sales@plumgarthsfoodservice.co.uk
www.plumgarths.co.uk

Availability: Farm shop on site.

Description: Plumgarths
Farmshop supplies locally reared
beef, lamb, pork and free range
eggs, as well as operating as a
distribution hub supplying 12 Asda
stores with 80 products from local
North West suppliers. They also
specialise in meat supply to hotels
and restaurants in the region.

Riley's Sausage

Carol Riley
9 Cornwall Street,
Openshaw, Manchester,
Greater Manchester M11 2WQ
phone 0161 231 1101
email info@rileysausage.co.uk
www.rileysausage.co.uk

Availability: Shop on site, mail
order, phone or fax orders.

Description: High quality
producers of the Riley sausage
and other sausage products
from their shop in Manchester.
Products also include a Halal
range and of course, the famous
'Manchester Sausage'.

Savin Hill Farm

Michelle Partington
The Barn, Savin Hill, Lyth Valley,
Kendal, Cumbria LA8 8DJ
phone 01539 568410
email food@savin-hill.co.uk
www.savin-hill.co.uk

Availability: Available online and
at Farmers' Markets and at NW
Fine Food Lovers Festivals.

Description: Savin Hill is home
to rare breed British White cattle
and Middle White pigs, both
traditional North English breeds.
They are slower maturing and
reared extensively on grass in
the Lake District. The result is a
meat that is marbled and tender,
with guaranteed taste, flavour
and quality.

The Scotch Beef Shop

Anthony Hayes
23 Woolton Street, Woolton Village,
Liverpool, Merseyside L25 5NH
phone 0151 428 1281
www.thescotchbeefshop.co.uk

Availability: Shop on site.

Description: Butchers of
distinction where customers come
again and again because they
can taste the difference. Along
with selling Premium Quality beef,
pork, lamb and free range poultry
they produce award winning
sausages, home cured bacon,
delicious black puddings and
home cooked meats. Member
of the Guild of Q Butchers.

DC Scott & Sons (Ormskirk) Ltd

Peter Scott
25-27 Church Street, Ormskirk,
Lancashire L39 3AG
phone 01695 572104

Availability: Butchers shop on site.

Description: Traditional high class butchers selling only the finest meat, and meat products sourced from local producers. The firm was established in 1923 and is now run by a third generation of the family who have supplied quality meat throughout West Lancashire for over three quarters of a century. They produce their own home cured bacon, sausages and brawn (Lancashire speciality).

Shaw Meats Ltd

Barry Shaw
Unit 1, Millers Business Park,
Station Road, Wigton,
Cumbria CA7 9BA
phone 01697 344328
email office@shawmeats.co.uk
www.shawmeats.co.uk

Availability: Farmers' markets, at NW Fine Food Lovers Festivals and mail order. See website for further details.

Description: Shaw Meats sell a wide range of Cumbrian salamis, also gluten free sausages and burgers, dry cured bacon products, wild venison and game, Cumbria Biltong and various other cuts of meat.

nwfinefoodawards 2007

Best SAUSAGE and Best SAUSAGE WITH NATURAL ADDITIVES

Fence Gate Inn

Pork, Leek, Black Pudding and Sage

This category includes plain meat sausage, sausages with natural additives, Cumberland sausage and black pudding. To qualify sausages must be produced in the North West using rgional produce wherever possible. The production process must be under the control or supervision of the producer. The judges were divided on the overall winner but eventually agreed that the Pork, Leek, Black Pudding and Sage Sausage was the overall winner, describing it as a "good well made sausage, excellent for a lunch menu". Fence Gate Inn is a beautifully restored three storey 17th Century building, with two banqueting suites and a modern brasserie under the watchful eye of owner, and former butcher, Kevin Berkins. The food operation is dedicated to using local produce and Kevin takes great pride in producing sausages and other local delicacies for the brasserie menu.

Kevin Berkins

Fence Gate Inn, Wheatley Lane Road, Fence, Nr Burnley, Lancashire BB12 9EE
phone 01282 618101
www.fencegate.co.uk

Availability: Currently only available on the menu at Fence Gate Inn.

Notes on sausages

The best selling cheap sausages usually have a mixture of 41% 'pork'. By law this description allows attached fat and connective tissue.

They also contain around 20% water, 10% pork fat, then an unappetising balance of rusk, potato starch, soya protein concentrate, salt, stabilisers, diphosphates, guar gum, antioxidants, sodium metabisulphate and cochineal, to give them a rather odd pink colour.

Such products are so processed and finely minced there is no texture at all, so fat is added to give the sausage a bit of 'bite', so that it feels like you're actually chewing something. If a packet of pork sausages doesn't say "reared outdoors", then it's likely to come from pigs reared in crowded factory conditions, sometimes 2,000 to a shed on concrete floors. They're packed together with little room to move and with such a lack of fresh air,

respiratory disease is high so they're routinely given antibiotics to keep them going. The taste of over-processing is salty and bland and the texture is horribly like blancmange.

An excellent pig breed for sausages is the Gloucestershire Old Spot, which were traditionally kept in orchards and fattened on the fruit that had blown from the trees. Their meat is well-marbled and sweet tasting. The best farms now feed their pigs on wheatgerm and good quality milk, and you can see the pigs roaming free. Their sausages have a meat content of between 80 - 95%, using prime shoulder and belly pork trimmed of fat. The remainder may be fresh herbs, wine or garlic, but definitely no preservatives and no colouring. The filling will look consistent all the way along its length with some texture, but no clumps of meat or fat and no air bubbles, and the skin will be slightly shiny.

Undoubtedly the best way to cook sausages is on a low heat, don't prick the skins, slowly in the oven (say 170°C for 45 minutes), they will brown perfectly and evenly, and the smell and the sizzle, let alone the taste, will be delicious. Now that's a true British banger.

nwfinefoodawards 2007

Best PLAIN MEAT SAUSAGE

Tatton Park, Housekeeper's Store
Pork Sausage

To qualify sausages must be produced in the North West using regional produce wherever possible. The production process must be under the control or supervision of the producer. The judges liked this plain Pork Sausage, complementing it on its moistness and describing it as having a "nice herbiness without being too strong". Tatton Park produce sausages, prime venison and lamb from animals reared in the Park's estate. The Housekeeper's Store in the Park sells all this estate reared produce and other products such as dry cured bacon.

Elizabeth Hough
Housekeeper's Store, Tatton Park, Knutsford, Cheshire WA16 6QN
phone 01625 534400
www.tattonpark.org.uk

Availability: Shop on site.

Sillfield Farm Products

Peter Gott
Sillfield Farm, Endmoor, Kendal,
Cumbria LA8 0HZ
phone 01539 567609
email enquiries@sillfield.co.uk
www.sillfield.co.uk

Availability: At farmers' markets and at Borough Market.

Description: Sillfield produce fresh wild boar and pork, speciality sausages, Cumberland ham, bacon and pies. They use traditional processes for their dry cured meats, air dried hams and unpasteurised cheeses. They also sell pedigree poultry.

Steadmans

Garth Steadman
2 Finkle Street, Sedbergh,
Cumbria LA10 5BZ
phone 01539 620431
www.steadmans-butchers.co.uk

Availability: Shop on site and wholesale to the trade.

Description: Steadmans stock a wide range of home made and local produce including quality meats, Aberdeen Angus beef, local Dales lamb, Garsdale pork, award winning dry cured bacon and hams including 'Parma style' air dried ham. Over 100 home made specialty sausages, burgers and pies. 'National Barbeque Award' winner. Member of the Guild of Q Butchers.

Tatton Park, Housekeeper's Store

Brendan Flanagan
and Elizabeth Hough
Tatton Park, Knutsford,
Cheshire WA16 6QN
phone 01625 534400
www.tattonpark.org.uk

Availability: Shop on site.

Description: Tatton Park produce prime venison from the estate, including steaks, medallions or joints, premium hot smoked venison, venison sausage and quality potted venison. Other products include dry cured bacon, pork, rare breed or Park reared lamb.

FB Taylor & Son Ltd

Frank Taylor
138 Northenden Road, Sale,
Cheshire M33 3HE
phone 0161 973 3480
www.taylorsbutchers.co.uk

Availability: Shop on site and wholesale to the trade.

Description: Since 1850 Taylor's butchers have been committed to quality meats and quality service. Sourced from local farms they maintain the strictest quality produce control. They offer a wide choice including homemade, award winning sausages and a lean cuisine range approved by Slimming World. Member of the Guild of Q Butchers.

Udale Handmade Pies

Kerry Pollard
Schola Green Lane, Morecambe,
Lancashire LA4 5QT
phone 01524 410519
email sales@udales.com
www.udale.com

Availability: Supply wholesale,
retail and to the catering trade.

Description: Udale Handmade
produce an award winning range
of speciality pies, pasties, sausage
rolls and fruit pies. Distribution is by
their own vans across the region
supplying wholesale, retail and
the catering trades.

Udale Speciality Foods

Ian & Neil Udale
Schola Green Lane, Morecambe,
Lancashire LA4 5QT
phone 01524 411611
email udale@udale.com
www.udale.com

Availability: Wholesale to
the trade.

Description: A long established
and traditionally run family
business manufacturing their
own Cumberland Sausage.
They specialise in supplying local
fresh meat, poultry, game and
regional fine foods to premier
hotels and restaurants throughout
the Lake District, North Lancashire
and surrounding areas.

Uppercrust Pie Co Ltd

John & Christine Lomas
50 Hardmans Road,
Whitefield, Manchester,
Greater Manchester M45 7BD
phone 0161 766 9744
email john@uppercrustpies.com
www.uppercrustpies.com

Availability: Wholesale to
farmshops and delicatessens,
and hampers online.

Description: Manufacturers and
distributors of traditional hand
raised pies which are available
in a variety of sizes and toppings.
They are members of the Rare
Breed Society and promote the
use of rare breed meat in pies.
Also distributors of niche products
to delis and farm shops and
suppliers of hampers promoting
traditional foods.

JT Vernon Ltd

Andrew Vernon
Fresh Food Hall, The Cross, Holt,
Wrexham, Wales LL13 9YG
phone 01829 270247
email sales@jtvernon.co.uk
www.jtvernon.co.uk

Availability: Food Hall including
impressive family butcher and
online ordering.

Description: A fresh Food Hall of
the highest standard. Situated just
on the border, they have held the
'Top Shop in Wales' award for two
years running and the 'Best
Butchers Shop in Wales' award.
Home made sausage and home
cured bacon. Member of the
Guild of Q Butchers.

David Wearden
Quality Fresh Foods

David Wearden
118 Poulton Road, Fleetwood,
Lancashire FY7 7AR
phone 01253 872636

Availability: Butchers shop on site.

Description: Traditional family run butchers selling a range of quality locally sourced meats, award winning speciality sausage, own cured bacon, own cooked meats and barbecue selection. Beef fully matured for 14 days. Gold Award winning sausages. Member of the Guild of Q Butchers.

Weatheroak Ostrich Farm

Kerry McNickle
Back Lane, Weeton, Preston,
Lancashire PR4 3HS
phone 01253 836386

Availability: Available for wholesale and also at food events and farmers' markets.

Description: Ostriches have been farmed at Weatheroak since 1995. The company produces quality ostrich products including meat, burgers, sausages, patés and pies. Ostrich is becoming increasingly well known as the healthy alternative to red meat as it is virtually fat free.

nwfinefoodawards
2007

Fence Gate Inn
Cumberland Sausage

To qualify sausages must be produced in the
North West using rgional produce wherever
possible. The production process must be under
the control or supervision of the producer. In a hotly
contested category, the Cumberland Sausage
winner went to a producer from outside Cumbria.
Lancashire's Fence Gate Inn won with a product
described by judges as having "good
Cumberland flavour" and a "nice classic taste".
Owner and former butcher, Kevin Berkins, serves
these home made sausages on his modern
brasserie menu. His food operation is dedicated
to using local produce and Kevin believes this
shines through in the taste. Our judges agree.

Kevin Berkins
Fence Gate Inn, Wheatley Lane Road, Fence,
Nr Burnley, Lancashire BB12 9EE
phone 01282 618101
www.fencegate.co.uk

Availability: Currently only available on the menu
at Fence Gate Inn.

Best
CUMBERLAND SAUSAGE

Richard Woodall Ltd

Richard & Colin Woodall
Lane End, Waberthwaite, Millom,
Cumbria LA19 5YJ
phone 01229 717237
email
admin@richardwoodall.co.uk
www.richardwoodall.co.uk

Availability: Available from
their own shop in Waberthwaite,
online via their website and
at food outlets both regionally
and nationally.

Description: Established in 1828
Woodalls produce a high quality
range of products using traditional,
specialist skills. They supply
traditional sausages, bacon, dry
cured and air-dried hams using
pork from their own farm where
animal welfare is paramount. They
hold a Royal Warrant to supply
Cumberland sausage, hams and
bacon to H.M.Queen Elizabeth II.

Woods Butchers of Knutsford

Steve Connor
34 Princess Street, Knutsford,
Cheshire WA16 6BN
phone 01565 633268

Availability: Butchers shop on site.

Description: Set in the centre of
historic Knutsford, they are a high
class traditional butcher's selling
speciality products. They also offer
award winning sausage, traditional
dry cure bacon and gammon.
All their meat is sourced locally
and slow matured for extra
flavour and tenderness.

The Worrall House Farm Larder

Diane Edwards
Worrall House Farm,
Flatmans Lane, Downholland,
Nr Ormskirk, Lancashire L39 7HW
phone 0151 527 1210
email
farmerted@farmerteds.com
www.farmerteds.com

Availability: Retail farmshop.

Description: An established farm shop selling their own grass fed Aberdeen Angus beef, home cured bacon, gammon and a large variety of handmade sausages, along with local pork, lamb, cornfed and free range chickens. A wide range of specialist condiments, apple juices, cheese, patés, pies and breads are also available.

nwfinefoodawards
2007

Best
BLACK
PUDDING

Pork Traders Oakwell Ltd
Oakwell Black Pudding

To qualify black puddings must be produced in the North West using rgional produce wherever possible. The production process must be under the control or supervision of the producer. You either love it, or hate it, but this traditional North West product, stirs up keen competition, with a great deal of pride at stake. This year the judges unanimously agreed on the winner, describing it as having a "balanced flavour and lovely texture". William Greives of The Daily Telegraph was particularly smitten saying "for me - just as it should be". Founded in 1916, the company use a secret recipe that has been handed down from generation to generation. The Oakwell Black Pudding is made from fresh pigs' blood, together with 100% natural ingredients, including pearl barley, barley flour, pork back fat and bacon trimmings. They have also won a silver medal in the Concours du Meilleur Boudin of the much prized French Confrerie des Chevaliers du Goute-Boudin.

Nancy McKee
Pork Traders Oakwell Ltd, Holt Lane, Netherby Industrial Estate, Liverpool, Merseyside L27 2TB
phone 0151 457 7437
www.porktraders.co.uk

Availability: Supplied to restaurants and retail grocers and butchers.

nwfinefood winner2007

Fish

Smoked fish and seafood
Prepared fish and seafood
Fresh fish and seafood

nwfinefoodawards 2007

Port of Lancaster Smokehouse
Naturally Smoked Boneless Kipper

The Best Fish category includes fresh, smoked or prepared fish and seafood. There was no question that this product should win this category and gain the prestigious Producer of the Year 2007 accolade for Port of Lancaster Smokehouse. The judges were unanimous in their praise for the moistness and flavour of their Naturally Smoked Boneless Kipper. To qualify it had to have been caught in coastal or fresh waters/bays of the region or processed within the region to add substantial value to the final product. As one judge put it, these kippers are "luscious visually with wonderful texture, subtle flavour and beautiful skin". Their shop is situated in the historic 18th Century Glasson Dock on the estuary of the River Lune just ten minutes away from junction 33 off the M6.

Michael Price
Port of Lancaster Smokehouse, West Quay, Glasson Dock, Nr Lancaster, Lancashire LA2 0DB
phone 01524 751493
www.glassonsmokehouse.co.uk

Availability: At food events and local farmers' marekts, mail order online and their own shop.

Notes on smoked fish

Fish was once the mainstay of families in the North West. The coastline and rivers were fished, and catches were eaten immediately or preserved by potting in butter or by smoking or salting.

Good smoked fish should allow the taste of the natural product to shine through, so you can actually taste the fish, with the smoke complementing and not hiding it. Smoked salmon, although widely available, is still a delicacy and comparatively expensive. It is gutted, split, salted and then smoked. Most smoked salmon is "cold smoked", at a temperature which allows the pores to open sufficiently to absorb the smoke but doesn't cook the fish. The wood used varies, and could be oak, beech or applewood to chippings from whisky barrels. The lighter the smoke, the more the flavour of the fish comes through, whereas whisky barrels or peat add a rich, distinctive flavour.

Some traditional smokehouses also "hot smoke" salmon. This is done by raising the temperature after the initial cold smoke, so that the fish cooks, becoming firm and flaky but moist, and can be cut into wedges.

Large operators sometimes don't smoke fish at all in the way you would imagine, but instead brush or spray it with a smoke flavouring, rushing the process to produce a cheaper product.

If you close your eyes and taste smoked fish carefully, you can tell those that have come from traditional smokehouses in the North West, smoked by hand with a wonderful savoury taste. Smoked salmon can be naturally pink or even dark red, but should be firm in texture, slightly oily but not slimy, and when it is cut should be slightly transparent and shiny. It should be fresh tasting and not too salty. Other smoked fish are just as good, including haddock, herring and mackerel.

nwfinefoodawards 2007

Best PREPARED FISH OR SEAFOOD

Cumbrian Seafoods
The Best Beer Battered Haddock

To qualify the fish or seafood had to have been caught in coastal or fresh waters/bays of the region or processed within the region to add substantial value to the final product. There was some debate among judges it was felt that haddock is such a beautiful fish that it doesn't need to be battered, however they were won over by this product's lovely flaky fish underneath the crisp batter on top. Established in 1997 Cumbrian Seafoods provide a range of fresh fish, shellfish, coated and added value seafood products to the region's supermarkets, and are dedicated to setting the industry standard for the sector. In 2004 its Hot Smoked Mackerel won a NW Fine Food Award.

Jeanette Wong
Cumbrian Seafoods, Solway Industrial Estate, Mayport, Cumbria CA15 8NF
phone 01900 819700
www.cumbrian-seafoods.co.uk

Availability: In most major supermarkets.

Brookside Products

Paul Agnew
Harbour View, Glasson Estate,
Maryport, Cumbria CA15 8NT
phone 01900 815757
email
info@brooksideproducts.co.uk
www.brooksideproducts.co.uk

Availability: Available to the
wholesale trade.

Description: Producers of the
finest smoked Scottish salmon,
which is authentically cold-
smoked over oak wood chips.
Brookside produce an
authentically traditional product
and are able to supply a wide
range of salmon related products
to suit customer requirements.

Fish Fanatics

Dan & Aga Redfern
New Smithfield House,
New Smithfield Market,
Manchester,
Greater Manchester M11 2WP
phone 08707 444110
email info@fishfanatics.co.uk
www.fishfanatics.co.uk

Availability: Online mail
order service.

Description: Family run
fishmonger, fanatical about their
fish, which is sold on the internet
through their nationally acclaimed
and award winning online shop.
Over 100 premium and often
locally sourced products including
organic and wild Dee salmon,
wild turbot, lobster, prawns, crab
and famous smoked delicacies.

Furness Fish, Poultry & Game Supplies

Les Salisbury and Claire Worrall
Moor Lane, Flookburgh,
Grange-over-Sands,
Cumbria LA11 7LS
phone 01539 559544
www.morecambebayshrimps.com

Availability: Own retail premises, mail order online, Borough Market and wholesale.

Description: Producers of Morecambe Bay Potted Shrimps, plus a wide selection of game, smoked meats, poultry, fish, pastries and desserts. Their shop is open weekdays.

Lakeland Seafoods Ltd

Kevin Harris
Dockside, Dock Street, Fleetwood,
Lancashire FY7 6NU
phone 01253 772656

Availability: Available to Trade.

Description: Suppliers of fresh and frozen seafood including Smoked Fish, Marinated Fish, Exotic Fish and Caviar.
All processing done to customers specifications. Delivery is available in their refrigerated vehicles.

Port of Lancaster Smokehouse

John, Pat & Michael Price
West Quay,
Glasson Dock, Nr Lancaster,
Lancashire LA2 0DB
phone 01524 751493
www.glassonsmokehouse.co.uk

Availability: Food events, mail order, online and own factory shop.

Description: Producers of superior grade smoked Scottish salmon, and well known for their smoked hams, bacon, cheese, trout, duck breast, chicken and game. They also provide a smoking service for companies and individuals, and have a factory shop.

Best
PRODUCERS
BY COUNTY

nwfinefoodawards
2007

Cheshire Producer of the Year
Tatton Park, Housekeeper's Store
Knutsford

Cumbria Producer of the Year
Farmersharp
Lindal-in-Furness

Greater Manchester Producer of the Year
Frasers Butchers
Bolton

Lancashire Producer of the Year
Johnson & Swarbrick
Preston

Merseyside Producer of the Year
Broughs of Birkdale
Southport

Cheshire
Apple
Juice

...mley

Beverages

Soft drinks

Alcoholic liqueurs

Beer

Tea

Coffee

nwfinefoodawards 2007

Best BEVERAGE and Best ALCOHOLIC BEER

Millstone Brewery
'Love Saves the Day' Beer

This category included soft drinks, alcoholic liqueurs and beers, tea and coffee. To qualify the beverage must be produced in the North West using regional produce wherever possible. The production process must be under the control or supervision of the producer. The judges were unanimous on the overall winner and were really impressed by this beer. Comments included "clean, wheaty beer" and "great product, with a light fruitiness". The Millstone Brewery is situated in Vale Mill, originally part of Mossley's cotton heritage, where they have been brewing beer since 2003. They use traditional malt and hops and their beers are full bodied, typically pale in colour, heavily late hopped for aromas, and with a range of balanced bitterness to suite a variety of palates. Shame this beer is only available in Manchester at the 'Love Saves the Day' deli.

Nick Boughton
Millstone Brewery, Unit 4, Vale Mill, Micklehurst Road, Mossley, Lancashire OL5 9JL
phone 01457 835835
www.millstonebrewery.co.uk

Availability: Supplied to pubs and restaurants in the region, visit website for more details.

Notes on beer

I am a truly dedicated wine drinker, but there are times when nothing but a cold glass of beer will do; watching live sport or sitting in a very hot Mediterranean sun are just two examples.

I'm not a fan, however, of the weedy, mass produced, carbonated water version of beer, that's so often over-hyped and over-priced and described as lager. They all taste remarkably similar to me. No, I like a small, but perfectly formed, half of real ale.

Real ale is a type of beer defined by its traditional production, known as "cask conditioned" beer. Basically the yeast is still present in the container from which the beer is served, although it will have settled to the bottom and isn't poured into the glass. Because the yeast is still alive, the process of fermentation continues so that when you order it, it's fresh and has a natural clean taste.

Essentially it's what fine food is all about. It's not processed or artificial, being made from fresh and natural ingredients such as hops, malted barley, water and yeast. It's British, tastes fantastic and literally has thousands of different tastes and flavours depending on the ingredients and the region from which it was made.

There are so many different beer styles, from chocolatey stouts to light floral golden ales, it's great to experiment and see which you prefer. It must not be served too cold as it loses its complex flavours, nor too warm as it quickly loses condition. It should be colourful and bright and I prefer the ones that have a thick and creamy head, through which you drink the beer underneath.

It is however, perfectly natural for some not to have a head at all, and for some (especially wheat) beers to be cloudy. Good real ales should be sweet at the front of your mouth, while the dry bitter flavour should dominate the back of your mouth as you swallow.

nwfinefoodawards 2007

Best SOFT DRINK

Mawsons Traditional Drinks
Sarsaparilla

To qualify the soft drink must be produced in the North West using regional produce wherever possible. The production process must be under the control or supervision of the producer. Mawson's Sarsaparilla is a traditional herbal drink, made with selected herbal ingredients which include ginger, liquorice and sarsaparilla root. It can be diluted with still or sparkling water, soda water or it can be served hot. You either love or hate this Sarsaparilla, and the judges loved it, marking it ahead of other entries such as fruit juices or other non-alcoholic beverages.

Nigel Mawson and Hannah Hughes
Mawsons Traditional Drinks, Unit 11a,
New Line Industrial Estate, Bacup,
Lancashire OL13 9RW.
phone 01706 874448
www.sarsaparilla.co.uk

Availability: At food markets and events across the region and numerous outlets nationwide, as well as online through their website.

Adams & Russell

Frank Eaton
58 Argyle Street South Birkenhead,
Merseyside CH41 9BX
phone 0151 647 4210
email
info@adamsandrussell.co.uk
www.adamsandrussell.co.uk

Availability: Available from farm shops, delis and coffee shops in the region. Regular exhibitors at NW Fine Food Lovers Festivals.

Description: Roasters of fresh coffee, bringing together the finest coffee beans from around the world and blending them freshly on a daily basis. They supply roasted beans for espresso and cappuccino machines, roasted and ground coffee for pour and serve filter coffee machines and for cafetieres to hotels, restaurants and coffee shops.

The Apple Orchard Juice Co Ltd

John Williams and John Sheard
The Lodge, Burton Road, Natland,
Kendal, Cumbria LA9 7XX
phone 01539 722276
email
info@theappleorchardjuicecompany.co.uk
www.theappleorchardjuicecompany.co.uk

Availability: Available from farm shops and delis throughout Cumbria and the NW region, and by mail order from their website.

Description: The Apple Orchard Juice Company produces apple juice that has been described as 'simply delicious'. Hand prepared and gently pasteurised, each bottle contains the juice of at least 1.5kg of freshly pressed Cumbrian British apples, where possible. A range of liqueurs (coffee, vanilla, chocolate, ginger and cinnamon) are also available.

J Atkinson & Co

Mandy Jackson, Sue & Ian Steel
12 China Street, Lancaster,
Lancashire LA1 1EX
phone 01524 65470
email ian@thecoffeehopper.com
www.thecoffeehopper.com

Availability: Available from their own shop in Lancaster, and online from their website.

Description: Tea and coffee specialists, roasting daily on vintage equipment. Currently restoring the Grasshopper Tea Warehouse to its former glory. This ancient Lancastrian institution was established in 1837, and is possibly the oldest continuously trading, family run independent retailer in the area.

Cains Brewery

Louise Bell
Stanhope Street, Liverpool,
Merseyside L8 5XJ
phone 0151 709 8734
email info@cainsbeers.co.uk.
www.cainsbeers.com

Availability: Available from their own pubs in Merseyside, from Asda and other supermarkets, and online from their website.

Description: Cains has a proud history. Everything they do is firmly aimed at ensuring that anyone who tries their beers is left in no doubt that they are a speciality product created for discerning drinkers. Cains Beers are the official beer of Liverpool's 2008 Capital of Culture.

nwfinefood awards 2007

Strawberry Bank Liqueurs
Blackberry Gin

To qualify the alcoholic liquer must be produced in the North West using regional produce wherever possible. The production process must be under the control or supervision of the producer. This category had a huge number of entries from damson gin producers in the region, but the judges voted this Blackberry Gin ahead of all others. Comments from judges included "good rich colour and nice consistency" and "a very good product". Strawberry Bank Liqueurs are based in the Lyth Valley and use fruit grown in their own orchards and other farms in the area. They also make Damson Gin, Sloe Gin and Strawberry Vodka.

Helen and Mike Walsh
Strawberrry Bank Liqueurs, Wood Yeat Barn, Crossthwaite, Kendal, Cumbria LA8 8HX
phone 01539 568812
www.damsongin.com

Availability: Available from food outlets in Cumbria and at food events in the region. For a full list of stockists visit their website.

Best
ALCOHOLIC LIQUEUR

Cockrobin Cider

Robin Barton
The Beeches, Kingside Hill, Wigton,
Cumbria CA7 4PN
phone 07989 592566
email robin@cockrobin.org
www.cockrobin.org

Availability: Available from
selected pubs in Cumbria, for
collection by appointment, from
local Farmers' Markets and Farm
Shops, and online mail order.

Description: Cockrobin Cider was
born out of a real cider draught in
the North of England, and from it's
initial success has grown to
produce three fine ciders, pressed
from Herefordshire cider fruit and
rare local fruit. They use a modern
belt press, combined with
traditional techniques, to produce
entirely natural beverages.
They also produce Wild
Elderflower Champagne.

Cowmire Hall Damson Gin

Oliver & Victoria Barratt
Crosthwaite, Kendal,
Cumbria LA8 8JJ
phone 01539 568200
www.cowmire.co.uk

Availability: Available from many
food outlets in Cumbria and the
UK, and online from Windemere
Wine Stores. For further details
and a full list of stockists, visit the
Cowmire Hall website.

Description: Cowmire Hall
Damson Gin is made in the
traditional way by steeping local
damsons in specially blended
London Gin. It is supplied in 50cl
and 25cl bottles at 26% ABV, and
sold wholesale by the case of 12
and 24 respectively. No artificial
ingredients. Also available,
Cowmire Hall Damson
Christmas Puddings.

Eddisbury Fruit Farm

Michael Dykes
Yeld Lane, Kelsall,
Cheshire CW6 0TE
phone 01829 751255
email m.dykes@eddisbury.co.uk
www.eddisbury.co.uk

Availability: Cheshire Apple Juice is available from many outlets throughout the region, at farmers' markets, and online, for further details visit their website.

Description: The home of Cheshire apple juice and cider. A family business since 1936 - growers of the finest quality fruit and vegetables on rich Cheshire soils. They also have a farm shop, 'pick your own' and guided production and orchard tours.

Exchange Coffee Company

Richard Isherwood
24 Wellgate, Clitheroe,
Lancashire BB7 2DP
phone 01200 442270
www.caffeine-rush.co.uk

Availability: Available from their coffee shops in Blackburn and Clitheroe and at food festivals across the region.

Description: The world's finest coffee roasted daily with over 50 coffees and 60 teas available in Victorian coffee houses in Blackburn and Clitheroe. Wholesale coffee supplied nationwide to restaurants, hotels, cafés, delis and pubs. Exchange Coffee are also cappuccino machine specialists.

MAWSON'S
EST.1933
SARSAPARILLA
CORDIAL
70th
2003
MAWSON'S
SARSAPARILLA
CORDIAL
MAWSON'S
DANDELION & BURDOCK
MAWSON'S
EST.1933
SARSAPARILLA
CORDIAL
to the original Sarsaparilla recipe
MAWSON'S
EST.1933
SARSAPARILLA

Lancashire Tea Company Ltd

Paul Needham and Lynn Hitchen
Unit 20, Deacon Trading Estate,
Newton-le-Willows,
Lancashire WA12 9XD
phone 01925 220333
email sales@lancashiretea.co.uk
www.lancashiretea.co.uk

Availability: Available from supermarkets, independent retailers, cafés and restaurants throughout the region. Visit their website for a full list of stockists.

Description: Manufacturers and distributors of Lancashire Tea - the way it should be! A high quality blend which is available in both teabag and loose tea format. Their customers include mutiples, wholesalers, independent retailers and hotels and caterers. Their products are available in a range of product sizes to suit all requirements. The tea is blended to a high specification and manufactured in a state of the art production facility.

Mawsons Traditional Drinks Ltd

Nigel Mawson
and Hannah Hughes
Unit 11a, New Line Industrial Estate,
Bacup, Lancashire OL13 9RW
phone 01706 874448
email info@sarsaparilla.co.uk
www.sarsaparilla.co.uk

Availability: Mawson's drinks can be bought at many food markets and events across the region and numerous outlets nationwide, as well as online through their website.

Description: Mawson's Sarsaparilla is a traditional herbal drink, made with selected herbal ingredients which include ginger, liquorice and sarsaparilla root. Dilute with still or sparkling water, soda water or enjoy hot in the winter months. Mawsons also produce Dandelion and Burdock and Cream Soda.

Moorhouses Brewery Ltd

David Grant
4 Moorhouse Street, Burnley,
Lancashire BB11 5EN
phone 01282 422864
email info@moorhouses.co.uk
www.moorhouses.co.uk

Availability: Moorhouses Brewery own six pubs of their own in Burnley, Bury, and Rawtenstall, and supply to around 300 free trade pubs within a 50 mile radius of the brewery site.

Description: Brewer of English Bitter Beers since 1978. Their products have won recognition at the Brewing Industry International Awards and The Champion Beer of Britain. Their Premier Bitter, Black Cat and Pendle Witches Brew have won numerous awards. Available in casks and bottles and distributed to pubs, clubs, restaurants and hotels throughout the country.

Paradise Brewing Company

John Wood
Ty Tan-y-Mynydd, Moelfre,
Abergele, Wales LL22 9RF
phone 0800 0834100

Availability: Available at farmers' markets, county shows and country fairs throughout the region.

Description: Bottle conditioned beers, presently brewed at Reddish, Stockport, Cheshire.

nwfinefoodawards 2007

Roberts & Co
Nicaragua Los Laureles

Best
COFFEE

To qualify the coffee must be roasted and packed in the North West. This Nicaragua Los Laureles coffee is well roasted with a full-bodied flavour which lingers in the mouth and down the back of the throat. Roberts & Co are suppliers of specialist coffees and teas to the catering and retail trades. They sell direct and by mail order from their roastery in Mawdesley, which incorporates a tasting and espresso bar. Using traditional roasters, which are on display in the roastery, they can produce coffee to suit every palate.

Amy and John Roberts
Roberts & Co, Cedar Farm, Back Lane, Mawdesley, Ormskirk, Lancashire L40 3SY
phone 01704 822433
www.e-coffee.co.uk

Availability: Available by mail order and at the Coffee Roastery. Also sold at the Café on Cedar Farm.

Notes on coffee

The coffee tree has a fruit known as cherries, which ripen from a green to a purple colour. The traditional story about the invention of today's coffee drink, is that it was first recognised in Ethiopia by a shepherd who noticed how his sheep were more alert after they'd eaten these cherries.

He begun eating them to give himself a buzz, but the local mystics believed that such pleasure was associated with the devil and threw them on the fire. The wonderful smell that resulted was enough to change their minds, and they begun adding them to hot water to make a wonderfully aromatic drink.

Good quality coffee is hand picked so that only the ripe cherries are used, but in cheaper coffee the whole branch of cherries is combined whether the berries are over-ripe or green. This is quicker and cheaper, but can lead to a bitter or burnt aftertaste. Each cherry has a skin, a pulp, a tough parchment and a thin silver skin.

These are removed to reveal the seeds (or beans) in the middle. Normally there are two seeds facing each other, and once harvested in this way they can keep for many years, some even improving in flavour. But it's when they're roasted that the oils and aromas are released.

Roasting essentially caramelises the natural sugars, with high-grown trees having bigger amounts of natural sugars and other aromatic flavours, which should not be over roasted so they retain their richer, more complex flavours. A good coffee, well roasted and harvested by hand will have a full-bodied flavour which lingers in the mouth and down the back of your throat.

Poor quality coffees have a flat flavour, which don't linger but finish quickly. Like wine, it's perfectly acceptable to blend different coffees, even from different countries, to obtain a mix of flavours, strength and character. The skill is not just in the harvesting of coffee, but in making complex decisions about the mix of beans, and the appropriate length of roast to give the final product.

Punch Brew Company

Jacqui Fildes
49 Queensway, Moss Bank,
St Helens, Merseyside WA11 7BY
phone 01744 600981
email enquiries@punchbrew.com
www.punchbrew.com

Availability: Available from farmers' markets, and food events throughout the region. Please call for further information.

Description: Lakeland Herbal Punch is prepared from an Olde Monastic recipe with twelve different herbs, made using traditional methods.
The mix is carefully chosen to give pleasure and aid relaxation just as nature intended.

Raw Juice Company

Neil Howarth and Jane Stokes
Goyt Mill, Upper Hibbert Lane,
Marple, Stockport,
Cheshire SK6 7HX
phone 0161 427 7800
email sales@rawjuice.biz
www.rawjuice.biz

Availability: Available in cafés, sandwich shops, restaurants etc throughout the region.

Description: Producers and suppliers of freshly squeezed citrus fruit juices, fruit smoothies, freshly prepared fruit salads, whole fruit and fruit purees to the catering trade. Their customers include hotels, cafés, restaurants, health clubs, sandwich bars, specialist vodka bars, ice cream manufacturers and bakers.

Roberts & Co

Amy & John Roberts
The Coffee Roastery,
Café @ Cedar Farm, Back Lane,
Mawdesley, Ormskirk,
Lancashire L40 3SY
phone 01704 822433
email roberts@e-coffee.co.uk
www.e-coffee.co.uk

Availability: Available by mail
order and at the Coffee Roastery.
Also sold at the Café on
Cedar Farm.

Description: Suppliers of specialist
coffees and teas to the catering
and retail trades. They sell direct
and by mail order from their
roastery in Mawdesley, which
incorporates a tasting and
espresso bar. Using traditional
roasters, which are on display in
the roastery, they can produce
coffee to suit every palate.

Strawberry Bank Liqueurs

Helen & Mike Walsh
Wood Yeat Barn, Crossthwaite,
Kendal, Cumbria LA8 8HX
phone 01539 568812
www.damsongin.com

Availability: Available from many
food outlets in Cumbria and the
UK, for a full list of stockists visit
their website.

Description: Producers of fruit
based liqueurs in the Lyth Valley
including Damson Gin, using fruit
grown in their own orchards and
other farms in the area. They also
sell Blackberry and Sloe Gins,
Blackberry Liqueur (whisky based)
and Strawberry Vodka, all made
with pure fruit juices.

Zest

Penny Bailey and Peter Slater
5 Holme Road,
Didsbury, Manchester,
Greater Manchester M20 2TX
phone 0161 445 9590

Availability: Available from their juice bar, at NW Fine Food Festivals and events across the region.

Description: Zest are an award winning juice bar situated in the heart of Manchester and are now regular traders at North West events. They serve the purest and freshest juices, smoothies, cocktails, liqueur coffees, hot and cold punches, strawberries and cream and fresh fruit salads.

nwfinefoodawards
2007

Lancashire Tea Company Ltd
Lancashire Leaf Tea

Best TEA

To qualify the tea must be blended and packed in the North West. This Lancashire Leaf Tea was described by the judges as having a "smooth palate" and "extremely refreshing". It was felt that this was a high quality blend which benefits from being in the loose tea format. Lancashire Tea Company sell to mutiples, wholesalers, independent retailers and hotels and caterers. The tea is blended to a high specification and manufactured in a state of the art production facility.

Paul Needham and Lynn Hitchen
Lancashire Tea Company, Unit 20,
Deacon Trading Estate, Newton-le-Willows,
Lancashire WA12 9XD.
phone 01925 220333
www.lancashiretea.co.uk

Availability: Available from supermarkets, independent retailers, cafés and restaurants throughout the region. Visit their website for a full list of stockists.

Chutneys and Preserves

Jam

Jelly

Marmalade

Chutney

Pickle

Mustard

Honey

Curd

nwfinefoodawards
2007

Best
CHUTNEY OR PRESERVE
and Best
CHUTNEY, PICKLE OR MUSTARD

Lizzie's Home Made
Cumbrian Frutta Cotta Mostarda

This category included jam, jellies, marmalade, chutney, pickle, mustard, honey and curds. To qualify the product must be produced in the North West using regional produce wherever possible. The judges immediately fell for this wonderful Cumbrian Frutta Cotta Mostarda, based on the traditional, voluptuous Italian condiment of fruit preserved in syrup that gains a kick from the addition of mustard. It not only won the best chutney, pickle or mustard, and the overall category, but was also voted New Product of the Year 2007. Judges loved the whole fruit, its innovation and slight quirkiness. Lizzie makes this from the finest ingredients using a selection of dried organic apricots, figs, prunes and dried cherries as the fruit base. Organic cane sugar and organic white wine vinegar make up the syrup with a touch of Vulcan honey mustard.

Elizabeth Smith
Lizzie's Home Made, The Bank, Dockray, Matterdale, Penrith, Cumbria CA11 0LG
phone 01768 482487
www.fruttacotta.co.uk

Availability: Retail and wholesale, the website details available stockists.

420g
LIZZIE'S
HOMEMADE
Cumbrian Mostar
Sweet mustard relish made with dried fruit
A relish to relish! Try with hot and cold meat.

Notes on jam and marmalade

The best jam is bright, fresh-looking, tastes of recently picked fruit and is not too sweet, it should burst with flavour and make the tip of your tongue tingle.

I love jam that has a natural dark red or nearly black colour, such as blackcurrants or damsons, all the better to contrast with the white colour of my farmhouse butter as it slowly melts underneath, and the feint brown of my lightly toasted hand-cut nutty bread. For a change marmalade has a slighter bitter edge of citrus, but for both I like the texture of fruit or peel, and don't really go for the smooth varieties with the pips taken out, as the mouth feel is too bland. Under European law the word marmalade can only be applied to fruit preserves made from citrus fruits, any other kind of fruit used must be called 'jam'.

Good jam and marmalade has a balance of sweetness against the clean, natural acidity of the fruit. You should be able to see pieces of the fruit used to make it, and the jelly should be clear as this shows it has been cooked slowly. It's important not to overcook jam. When boiling it needs to be watched very carefully as it quickly reaches setting point, and can easily end up as stiff and overcooked. In this state it loses its colour, taking on a feint brown hue and a flavour of caramel, it can actually smell burnt. If it's too dry and hard to spread this is a sign that too much sugar has been used.

Jams set because of the action of pectin, a substance in fruit that, when cooked with sugar and acid (from the fruit), thickens and sets. Good jam, jelly or marmalade uses fruit that is in peak condition, preferably slightly under ripe, picked just before late autumn. The pectin in over-ripe or damaged fruit begins to change to pectose and will not set well, although they do make good chutneys. But with jam, the final product is likely to deteriorate rapidly.

nwfinefoodawards
2007

Best JAM,
JELLY OR
MARMALADE

Herbs and Preserves
Finest Blackcurrant Jam

To qualify the product must be produced in the
North West using regional produce wherever
possible. This Finest Blackcurrant Jam was a clear
winner, with a deep fruit taste and excellent texture.
The judges commented that the jam was
traditional and had a "good balance" and
"incredible flavour". Karen grows fresh herbs for
cooking and planting out and makes homemade
jams, marmalades, chutneys and curds using fresh
local produce wherever possible, with no artificial
additives or ingredients.

Karen Challinor
Herbs and Preserves, Rushey Hey, Oak Lane,
Astbury, Congleton, Cheshire CW12 4RT
phone 07766 104416

Availability: Available at farmers' markets
in Cheshire.

AS Greek Olives

Ahmed Asadi
Flat 9, Ellinshaw Row,
Eccles New Road, Salford,
Greater Manchester M5 4UJ
phone 0161 743 9441

Availability: NW Fine Food Lovers Festivals and farmers' markets.

Description: A S Olives sell Greek delicatessen olives, feta cheese and sun dried tomatoes ready for the market in containers. Some of the olives are presented in their delicious own home made sauces.

Cheshire Cottage Preserves

Mike Turner
Minara House,
Leestone Road, Manchester,
Greater Manchester M22 4RB
phone 07748 120521
email
cheshirecottage@hotmail.co.uk

Availability: NW Fine Food Lovers Festivals, farmers' markets and major supermarkets.

Description: Producers of extra fruit jams and preserves with no colour or preservatives, using local fruit wherever possible. New developments include a sugar-free range and an organic range.

Claire's Handmade

Claire Kent
Newlands House, Mealsgate,
Wigton, Cumbria CA7 1AB
phone 01697 371567
email
claire@claireshandmade.co.uk
www.claireshandmade.co.uk

Availability: Mail order and independent high quality food outlets.

Description: Producer of 'Best Overall Preserve' in the NW Fine Food Awards 2005 for Beetroot Chutney with Fresh Ginger. Claire and Michael produce premium preserves all handmade using traditional methods and no artificial ingredients. The range includes chutneys, jams, marmalades and a wonderful piccalilli.

Clippy's Apple Preserves

Michelle McKenna
PO Box 366, Sale,
Cheshire M33 4YH
phone 07753 838928
email apples@clippys.com
www.clippys.com

Availability: Mail order and independent high quality food outlets.

Description: Clippy's Apple Preserves was established in order to protect our native apple orchards. Clippy's are dedicated to working closely with local and regional orchards and suppliers. Clippy's passion for apples has produced a number of delicious preserves by combining Bramley Seedling Cookers and soft fruits.

Corrykinloch UK Limited

Anthony Sawyer
189 Manchester Road,
Oldham, Lancashire OL8 4PS
phone 0161 622 1389
email sales@corrykinloch.com
www.corrykinloch.com

Availability: Online mail order and trade.

Description: At Corrykinloch they believe in, and commit to, furnishing their customers with the best quality products and service possible at a fair price. All their products, seasonings, relishes, jellies and condiments are made with the freshest ingredients available.

Demels

Howard Wilson and John Tiscornia
Cross Lane Ulverston,
Cumbria LA12 9DQ
phone 01229 580580
email sales@demels.co.uk
www.demels.co.uk

Availability: NW Fine Food Lovers Festivals, farmshops and selected outlets and online.

Description: One of Rick Stein's Food Heroes, Demels produce a range of Award Winning Sri Lankan recipe chutneys, pickles and curry powders. Only quality natural ingredients are used. Since 2001 the exceptional quality of Demels products has been recognised every year, winning Great Taste 'Gold' Awards and NW Fine Food Producer of the Year Awards in 2002 and 2003.

Edmund Barton Ltd

Joanna Jenner
Lascelles Street, St Helens,
Merseyside WA9 1BA
phone 01744 22593
email
joanna@bartonspickles.com
www.bartonspickles.com

Availability: Major supermarkets, local grocers and delicatessens.

Description: It is no exaggeration to call Bartons Pickles a local legend; producing time-honoured British quality pickle recipes full of fantastic flavours and textures. Bartons is known for buying and selling locally, and was honoured by Prince Charles when HRH visited Bartons factory to celebrate 100 years of traditional family pickle making.

Friendly Food and Drink

Geoff Monkman
and Lorraine Stobbart
Crookes Farm, Bouth, Nr Ulverston,
Cumbria LA12 8JL
phone 01229 861112
email
info@friendlyfoodanddrink.co.uk

Availability: Delicatessen and farmshops. Mail order also available.

Description: A range of preserves, chutneys, coulis and bakery products which are suitable for the health conscious, diabetics or those with allergies. None of their products contain cane sugar, alternatives such as fruit sugar are used instead.

Gift of Oil

Phil Bianchi
The Enterprise Centre,
Washington Street, Bolton,
Lancashire BL3 5EY
phone 01204 559555
email
philbianchi@thegiftofoil.co.uk
www.thegiftofoil.co.uk

Availability: NW Fine Food Lovers Festivals, mail order and online.

Description: Superb single estate, family produced extra virgin olive oil from Puglia, Sicily, Catalonia and Lesbos and genuinely matured balsamic vinegar from Modena. Bottled, labelled and boxed in presentation packs in the North West.

Hawkshead Relish Company

Mark & Maria Whitehead
The Square Hawkshead,
Cumbria LA22 0NZ
phone 01539 436614
email info@hawksheadrelish.com
www.info@hawksheadrelish.com

Availability: Buy online - see website for further information.

Description: Award winning handmade Relishes, Pickles and Preserves, with no artificial flavourings, colourings or preservatives. Hawkshead have won dozens of Great Taste Awards and NW Fine Food Producer of the Year.

Honeycomb Company Ltd

Paul & Margaret Humphreys
Pennine Bee Farm,
Stoney Lane, Ellel Lancaster,
Lancashire LA2 0QY
phone 01524 751347
www.honeycombcompany.co.uk

Availability: Selected outlets,
see website and own factory
showoom at Galgate.

Description: Honeycomb English
honey is marketed under the
Pennine Bee Farm label and this
range, which is constantly being
extended, includes unusual
honeys and a selection of pottery
items for the gift trade. The
company also has an extensive
range of quality preserves and
handmade biscuits all made
to their own recipes.

Lizzie's Home Made

Elizabeth Smith
The Bank, Dockray Penrith,
Cumbria CA11 0LG
phone 01768 482487
www.fruttacotta.co.uk

Availability: Retail and
wholesale, the website details
available stockists.

Description: Lizzie's Home Made
make two Frutta Cottas.
'Cumbrian' is a luxurious pudding
made of organic dried apricots,
figs and prunes in a spiced rum
syrup, using 'Jefferson's', a local,
fine dark rum. 'Mastarda' is a
voluptuous relish made with
organic dried apricots, figs and
prunes with fat glace cherries to
give a crunch against the organic
white wine vinegar and Vulcan
honey mustard.

Notes on chutney and pickles

Summer plates of bread and cheese, or charcuterie or paté, work well with the injection of the salty sour addition of a pickle that releases flavour explosively as soon as you bite it.

I cannot eat paté without cornichons, so that the silky meat texture contrasts with the crunchy bite that only just stops short of making your eyes water. Pickles are generally any food preserved in acid, vinegar or salt. It is usually based on whole vegetables, and contains little or no sugar.

Pickle is a broad term that can include olives, piccalilli, beetroot, onions and cucumber. Freshly picked vegetables can be preserved for a long time by putting them in a brine that contains around 10% salt. The process stops the vegetables from degrading but allows the inherent sugars to ferment and produce lactic acid.

Once lactic fermentation is complete the original brine is replaced by another fresher brine which can contain herbs, flavourings etc. Some vegetables are preserved straight away by pickling in vinegar which can often make them too acidic. I prefer the ones that have been through lactic fermentation as the taste is more subtle.

Chutneys are a more refined, slower release taste. They are likely to be based on chopped fruit, spices and herbs and to contain more sugar. Whilst under-ripe fruit is good for jam making, over-ripe fruit can be good for making chutney, although the fruit itself must not be of inferior quality or have spoiled. Chutneys are often hot and spicy and based on fruits that have been boiled. They contain both sugar and vinegar giving that uniquely sweet and sour taste, and they should be coarse in texture. Often the major fruit has been preserved in the same way as a pickle, and is added during the cooking process. Whilst spicy hot chutneys are great with an Indian meal, there are good subtle varieties with bags of competing tastes that also go well with that plate of cheese and bread.

Pasco Spices and Herbs

Maggam & Seema Khade
and Farid Yousef
Pasco House, Makerfield Way,
Ince Wigan, Lancashire WN2 2PR
phone 01942 493220
email sales@pascospices.co.uk
www.pascospices.co.uk

Availability: Wholesale.

Description: Pasco is a small, creative family company which began making Indian curries in their own kitchen in 1992. They now manufacture a range of hot and mild curry dishes, hot, sweet and mild pickles and mouth watering chutneys, delicious dressings and relishes.

Perivoli UK Limited

Joanna & Ruth Wharton
Unit 5, Borrowdale Business Park,
Whitegate Morecambe,
Lancashire LA3 3BS
phone 01524 751702
email ask@perivoli.plus.com

Availability: Wholesale and retail.

Description: Perivoli prepares Mediterranean style foods, including marinated olives and dips made to traditional family recipes. The best fresh ingredients are used for exciting flavours and visual appeal. Importers of 'Dimitris' Greek honey, herbs and pulses.

Posh Pickles and Preserves

Stephanie Bath
23 Smithy Lane, Kingsley
Frodsham, Cheshire WA6 8ED
phone 01928 731603
www.poshpickles.com

Availability: Wholesale and online mail order.

Description: Posh Pickles and Preserves are quality, unique products, handmade in small batches to maintain an individual, impeccable flavour. Their diverse range of jams, chutneys, oils and relishes are completely free from additives and preservatives. Only high quality ingredients sourced from the local area go into their products.

Sue Prickett

Sue Prickett
Hutton Roof Hall, Hutton Roof,
Carnforth, Lancashire LA6 2PG
phone 01524 271435
email sue.prickett@bigfoot.com

Availability: NW Fine Food Lovers Festivals and agricultural shows. Kitridding Farm Shop, Kirkby Lonsdale.

Description: A small producer providing a quality product. All their preserves are homemade in small batches in their farmhouse kitchen, using local produce where possible. In 2004 they were awarded North West Supreme Champion, Producer of the Year at the NW Fine Food Awards.

Wild and Fruitful

Jane Maggs
Hillside, Cuddy Lonning, Wigton,
Cumbria CA7 0AA
phone 01697 344304
www.wildandfruitful.co.uk

Availability: Wholesale to
small delicatessens and
Westmorland Services.

Description: Homemade award
winning jams and preserves made
primarily with Cumbrian ingredients,
either from the wild or from
farmers, growers and private
gardens. All local ingredients
are traceable, with source stated
on each jar. They were awarded
Joint Supreme Champion NW Fine
Food Producer of the Year 2003.

nwfinefoodawards 2007

W&EF Neale
Lemon Curd

To qualify the product must be produced in the North West using regional produce wherever possible. Although there were a number of honeys and curds entered in this category, Freda Neale's Lemon Curd was outstanding. The judges described it as "excellent in every way", and Hannah Waring from Booths thought it had a "lovely tangy and buttery taste". For generations the Neale family have been farming in the heart of rural West Lancashire, with the best of their traditionally grown vegetables available at their farm shop along with their own chutneys, jams, pickles and preserves.

Freda Neale
W&EF Neale, The Farm, Martin Lane, Burscough, Ormskirk, Lancashire L40 0RT.
phone 01704 892247

Availability: Available from their farm shop and at farmers' markets in Lancashire and Merseyside.

Best
HONEY OR CURD

Prepared meals

Soups
Sauces
Terrines and patés
Pies
Savoury pastries
Seasonings and ingredients
Vegetarian meals

nwfinefoodawards 2007

Best
**PREPARED
MEAL and**
Best
**READY MEAL
OR PIE**

Broughs Butchers Birkdale
Lancashire Hot Pot

This category included soups, sauces, terrines, patés, potted meats, ready to eat meals, pies, savoury pastries and vegetarian products. To qualify the product must be produced in the North West using regional produce wherever possible, and must not contain hydrogenated fats, artificial colourings or flavourings. With a huge number of high quality entries in a wide ranging category it was difficult to choose a winner, but the judges eventually decided on Broughs of Birkdale's Lancashire Hot Pot. This was some achievement when so many good pies from the region had been entered. They were impressed by this ready meal's sweetish, spicy after taste and the quality of the ingredients. But what made it the overall winner is best summed up by the judges comments - "attractive thoughtful meal" and it "tastes and looks as though there has been a lot of tender loving care in its preparation". The Birkdale establishment thoroughly deserve this award because they use traditional values in the preparation of their meals and meat. If you get time you should visit the shop as it's an excellent example of the 'traditional' butchers featuring an original 'pay office' and the Victorian tiled walls.

David Allen
Brough Butchers, 20 Liverpool Road, Birkdale,
Southport, Merseyside PR8 4AY
phone 01704 567073
www.broughs.com

Availability: Shop on site.

Notes on terrines and patés

Patés and terrines are generally based on chopped or minced pork, often with a proportion of liver and sometimes including bacon. In the past, terrines remained in the container in which they were baked, whilst patés were turned out for serving.

This distinction has largely been eroded and now there isn't really any differentiation between the two terms.

Originally British recipes were devised to preserve pork, beef or game birds by first baking them and then sealing them with fat or butter. The cooked meat is used to make a smooth or rough purée with butter and mace or nutmeg. Sometimes brandy, rum or calvados was added, or the meat was combined with herbs, pork belly, bacon and liver. Bacon is useful in that it adds a pinkness to the colour, which helps as some patés can end up looking quite grey. I also like the slight edge of saltiness that the bacon adds. Butter is used to seal the meat which gives the paté or terrine a naturally long life without added preservatives.

Good patés and terrines should contain a decent amount of natural fat to bring out the flavour of the meat, which should taste well matured and moist. Smooth patés suit fish and liver based recipes, especially chicken liver paté made with a little drop of added brandy; an incredibly cheap dish to make. But for me, a paté made of meat generally works better as a rougher texture - thick and chunky with a meaty flavour that is well seasoned but not too rich. Bad patés and terrines are over-fatty, crumbly or dry, and can contain thickening agents, flavouring oils, milk fats and monosodium glutamate which contribute to a suspiciously long shelf life.

Patés and terrines should be kept well chilled and wrapped, and are excellent served with pickles, a great hunk of beautifully baked bread and a glass of red wine.

nwfinefood awards 2007

Best SOUP

Jeremy's Soups
Pea and Ham

To qualify the product must be produced in the North West using regional produce wherever possible, and must not contain hydrogenated fats, artificial colourings or flavourings. There were many soups submitted in this category, and the judges were looking for good consistency with the ingredients coming through strongly in the flavour. Appearance is also key to the appeal. This Pea and Ham soup was judged the overall winner by some margin. It "tastes superb" said one of the judges while Emily Shamma of Tesco described it as "excellent". Jeremy's Soups produce a range of fresh soups and sauces using traditional methods and the best local produce. They don't use any artificial colourings, flavourings, preservatives or MSG, and all are gluten free.

Jeremy & Helen Kent
Jeremy's Soups, Unit 4, Appleby Business Park, Drawbriggs Lane, Appleby-in-Westmorland, Cumbria CA16 6HX.
phone 01768 353311

Availability: Wholesale to restaurants. NW Fine Food Lovers Festivals and selected farmshops in the region

Carr's Flour

Caroline Dale
Old Croft, Stanwix, Carlisle,
Cumbria CA3 9SB
phone 01228 554600
email
caroline.dale@carrs-flourmills.co.uk
www.carrs-flourmills.co.uk

Availability: Retail and wholesale, available in upmarket delis, Booths, Sainsbury's and Asda.

Description: Carr's have milled wheat and produced top quality flours for 175 years with the care, skill and expertise that makes them first choice for many of the UK's leading craft bakers. They produce a comprehensive range of retail flours from plain and self raising, to the Breadmaker range and Delia's favourite Breadmaker Blends and Sauce Flour.

Essential Cuisine

Neil Corlett
Browning Way,
Woodford Park Industrial Estate,
Winsford, Cheshire CW7 2RH
phone 0870 050 1133
email neil@essentialcuisine.com
www.essentialcuisine.com

Availability: Supplied to the trade.

Description: Essential Cuisine produce a comprehensive range of quality stocks, bouillons, jus and glacés for the discerning chef. With the taste and performance of the best kitchen-made stocks their products are used with confidence by hotels, restaurants, pubs and caterers as well as farm shops and food manufacturers.

Food By Breda Murphy

Breda Murphy
Clough Bottom, Bashall Eaves,
Clitheroe, Lancashire BB7 3NA
phone 01200 448297
www.foodbybredamurphy.com

Availability: On site shop.

Description: Food by Breda
Murphy, offers quality foods
beautifully cooked and presented
for bespoke, contract catering,
home deliveries, private dining
and demonstration cooking.
The range includes jams,
marmalades and chutneys, made
free of additives and preservatives
and using organic fruits.

The Foodie Farmer
Fresh Soup Co

Richard Morphett
Cowside Farm,
Blackshawhead, Hebden Bridge,
West Yorkshire HX7 7JU
phone 01422 845952

Availability: Available from
farmers' markets in Manchester
and Lancashire.

Description: The Foodie Farmer
make fresh soups produced
from their own and local
ingredients. They grow most of
their own vegetables including
potatoes, carrots, onions and
herbs and source the majority
of other ingredients from local
farmers' markets.

nwfinefoodawards 2007

Best
SAUCE

Pasco Spices and Herbs
Jalfrezi Sauce

To qualify the product must be produced in the North West using regional produce wherever possible, and must not contain hydrogenated fats, artificial colourings or flavourings. The judges loved this Jalfrezi Sauce with Gordon Clark of the Restaurant Association saying it "looked good and tasted very good". Pasco is a small, creative family company which began making Indian curries in their own kitchen in 1992. They now manufacture a range of hot and mild curry dishes, hot, sweet and mild pickles and mouth watering chutneys, delicious dressings and relishes.

Maggam & Seema Khade and Farid Yousef
Pasco Spices and Herbs, Pasco House, Makerfield Way, Ince Wigan, Lancashire WN2 2PR
phone 01942 493220
www.pascospices.co.uk

Availability: Wholesale to the trade only.

Hartleys Farm Foods Ltd

Michael Hartley
Unit 1, Pendleside Lomeshaye
Business Park, Nelson,
Lancashire BB9 6RY
phone 01282 691700
email
michael@bigsandwich.co.uk
www.bigsandwich.co.uk

Availability: On site shop and
to the trade.

Description: Producers of award
winning cooked meats. The range
includes beef, ham, turkey,
chicken, and pre-sliced cooked
meats and sandwich fillings, such
as Chicken Tikka and Minty Lamb.
A 100% British range with 100%
traceability to farm of origin.

Jeremy's Soups

Jeremy & Helen Kent
Unit 4, Appleby Business Park,
Drawbriggs Lane,
Appleby-in-Westmorland,
Cumbria CA16 6HX
phone 01768 353311
email
jeremyssoups@ukonline.co.uk

Availability: Wholesale to
restaurants. NW Fine Food Lovers
Festivals and selected farmshops
in the region.

Description: Jeremy's soups
produce a range of fresh soups
and sauces using traditional
methods and the best local
produce. They don't use any
artificial colourings, flavourings,
preservatives or MSG, and all
are gluten free.

L&L's Company

Linda Myers
5 Daisyfields, Higher Bartle, Preston, Lancashire PR4 0AD
phone 01772 723652

Availability: Wholesale to restaurants. NW Fine Food Lovers Festivals and selected farmshops in the region.

Description: L&L's produce duck products such as duck fat, duck confit, duck, chicken and pork rillette. All made from the locally famous Goosnargh ducks, with all pork sourced from local suppliers.

Laila's Fine Foods

Laila & Alnazir Remtulla
Units 4 and 5, Lidun Industrial Park, Boundary Road, Lytham St. Annes, Lancashire FY8 5HU
phone 01253 732121
email enquiries@lailasfinefoods.co.uk
www.enquiries@lailasfinefoods.co.uk

Availability: Mail order online and to the trade.

Description: Laila's Fine Foods is a highly respected family run business producing hand prepared ready meals from specially trained chefs. Choose from their extensive range of eastern and western dishes, prepared using only the finest and freshest ingredients and mixed with their own spices.

nwfinefoodawards
2007

Best PATÉ
OR TERRINE

Not awarded

In the past this category has seen some excellent contenders, but the judges this year were disappointed that none of the entries were of the very high quality expected. We know there are some great patés and terrines being made out there in th North West, make sure they get entered next year for this category!

Linda's Souperior Soups

Linda Edwards
8 Links Close, Wallasey,
Merseyside CH45 0NH
phone 07772 462502
www.souperiorsoups.co.uk

Availability: NW Fine Food
Lovers Festivals and regional
farmers' markets.

Description: Producer and
supplier of a range of hand
made fresh soups, using the best
local and seasonal ingredients
wherever possible. The soups
are produced with health benefits
in mind and help to go towards
the 'five a day' requirement. No
artificial colourings, preservatives
or msg are used in the production,
which are suitable for vegetarians,
gluten and dairy free.

Lune Valley Real Foods

David Maiden
162 Dock Street, Fleetwood,
Lancashire FY7 6SB
phone 01253 773073

Availability: Available in retail
outlets and restaurants throughout
the region. Please call for
further information.

Description: Producers of
beautiful handmade frozen
gourmet pork pies and quiches.
They thaw to a perfect fresh
product that is begging to be
eaten. Pies are open and filled
with their own delicious relish
or relish and cheese.

Quay Ingredients

Deana Southworth
Low Laithe Barn, Wigglesworth,
Skipton, North Yorkshire BD23 4RQ
phone 01729 840740
email info@quayingredients.co.uk
www.quayingredients.co.uk

Availability: Wholesale and retail
at NW Fine Food Lovers Festivals
and mail order online.

Description: Quay Ingredients
offers an extensive range of fine
quality dried herbs, spices,
seasonings, speciality mushrooms,
sun dried tomatoes and peppers.
From the very best Hungarian
Noble Sweet Paprika to the finest
quality Madagascan Vanilla pods,
these speciality ingredients are
packed at Quay Ingredients in
the North West.

Seasoned Pioneers

Mark Steene and Matt Webster
Unit 8, Stadium Court,
Plantation Business Park,
Bromborough, Wirral,
Cheshire CH62 3RP
phone 0151 343 1122
email
info@seasonedpioneers.co.uk
www.seasonedpioneers.co.uk

Availability: Wholesale and retail,
at NW Fine Food Lovers Festivals
and online via the website.

Description: Highly commended
by many of the most credible UK
food writers - authenticity underpins
their gourmet cooking sauces.
They only use the finest ingredients
and dry-roast their entire range of
spice blends in-house using only
traditional methods and strictly
original recipes.

nwfinefoodawards 2007

Best COLD MEAT PIE OR SAVOURY PASTRY

The Little Farmhouse Bakery
Peppered Steak Pie

To qualify the product must be produced in the North West using regional produce wherever possible, and must not contain hydrogenated fats, artificial colourings or flavourings. Of all the cold pies and pastries submitted, this Peppered Steak Pie stood out for the judges. Mark Holdstock the presenter of Farming Today was a particular fan - "good rich flavour and taste". Other judges loved its richness and meatiness.

The Little Farmhouse Bakery is run by Raymond and Jill Tyson. It has a small bakery and a farm shop selling wonderful pies, homemade bread and delicious cakes and pastries.

Jill Tyson
The Little Farmhouse Bakery, Cuncliffe Fold Farm, Blackleach Lane, Salwick, Preston PR4 0RY
phone 01772 690622

Availability: At their own farm shop in Salwick.

Seasoners Fine Foods Ltd

Stephen Muller
The Old Peeling Station,
Moston Road, Middleton Junction,
Manchester,
Greater Manchester M24 1SF
phone 0161 643 9600
www.seasoners.co.uk

Availability: Wholesale.

Description: The company aim
is to produce the finest range of
pickles, preserves and sauces
available. They are truly proud of
their products and use traditional
methods and only the best
fresh ingredients.

So Baby Ltd

Sarah Dennison and Chris Larkin
Holly Cottage, Burwardsley Road,
Tattenhall, Chester,
Cheshire CH3 9NS
phone 07887 503486
email info@so-baby.co.uk
www.so-baby.co.uk

Availability: Buy online or by
telephone for next day delivery,
or at selected retail outlets.

Description: Producer and
supplier of delicious handmade
baby meals. 100% organic and
Soil Association certified. Using
only the finest and freshest local
ingredients, all meals are hand
prepared in small batches.

Notes on pies

Pastry is a pretty good foodstuff in its own right: A crisp edifice which melts and deconstructs as soon as it's put in your mouth, and gives a satisfyingly naughty feeling of destruction.

The idea of using this as a case to house meat so that it could be transported or stored easily, was nothing short of genius. Of course there is the hot version with gravy and well-cooked moist meat that barely needs chewing, all inside a soft crisp pastry that gives a crunch, but it is the raised pies served hot, but usually cold, that are a peculiarly British invention.

Raised pies are generally pork or game pies, and are made from a hot water crust that needs to be raised or moulded into shape. The best pies have that satisfying melt in the mouth, should be crisp on the outside and softer on the inside, but not soggy, with a beautiful golden colour that is nowhere near burnt.

It should envelope a good amount of meaty jelly and a chunky pork filling lightly seasoned. The meat should be minced pork with a high content of fat or coarsely minced dark game meat interspersed with layers of breast meat. A highly flavoured and seasoned stock made from the bones of the meat mixed with gelatine should be poured into the spaces left by shrinkage after cooking, thus adding to the fabulous meat flesh taste.

Badly made pork or game pies, do not use good quality meat, and a lack of naturally flavoured stock, often leads to a bland meat taste. Then of course there is that awful whitish raw pastry layer, between the over cooked crisp outside crust and the meat, not to mention the synthetic jelly whose texture jars in your mouth. Better off hunting for the real thing.

TeenyWeanies (Baby Food) Ltd

Sarah Farrow
68 Norwich Road,
Stretford, Manchester,
Greater Manchester M32 9TY
phone 0161 610 6638
email sarah@teenyweanies.co.uk
www.teenyweanies.co.uk

Availability: Availability shown on their website.

Description: TeenyWeanies is a brand new range of freshly frozen organic baby food specially cooked for children from four months old. Packed with the most seasonal organic fruit and vegetables, they help start the weaning process and can be used to help older children meet their 5-A-Day.

nwfinefoodawards
2007

Moody Baker
Carrot and Almond Nut Loaf

To qualify the product must be produced in
the North West using regional produce wherever
possible, and must not contain hydrogenated fats,
artificial colourings or flavourings. Although there
were a number of dedicated meat eating judges
on the panel, they were all agreed that this
vegetarian product was a clear winner. It was
described as having a nice slight crunch, and
of being "very pleasant". The Moody Baker bakery
is situated in the very pretty market town of Alston,
high up in the Cumbrian hills. It is an artisan bakery
owned by a workers' co-operative committed to
organic and local ingredients, with an impressive
range of wholefood and vegetarian products.
They make delicious breads, cakes, pies, quiches
and vegetarian and meat savouries. It is also
home to the original high-energy Moody Baker
Biker Bar.

Jesse Reid
Moody Baker, 3 West View, Alston,
Cumbria CA9 3SF
phone 01434 382003

Availability: From the bakery in Alston.

Best
VEGETARIAN PRODUCT

Fresh produce

Fruit
Vegetables
Salads
Herbs

nwfinefoodawards
2007

Best
FRESH PRODUCE

These awards are judged quarterly across the year, to take into account seasonality. Of this season's entries the judges particularly commended the following three products.

H&P Ascroft
Golden Beetroot
Purple Carrots

The Ascroft family have been farming the land around Holmes in Lancashire since the turn of the century. Against the modern trend of monoculture (growing one crop only) they have chosen to stick to the traditional way of growing a variety of arable crops in rotation so that the goodness stays in the soil and pests and diseases are kept to a minimum.

Peter Ascroft
H & P Ascroft, Worthingtons Farm, Park Lane, Tarleton, Nr. Preston, Lancashire PR4 6JN.
phone 01772 814465

Availability: Available to the trade.

Wareings
January King Cabbage

Run by Clive and Debbie Wareing and featured on ITV'S Grubs Up programme, this family farm produces wonderful vegetables such as celeriac, purple sprouting broccoli, pink fir apple potatoes and Swiss ruby chard, and of course this wonderful January King Cabbage.

Debbie Wareing
Johnsons Farm, Johnsons Meanygate, Tarleton, Preston, Lancashire PR4 6JN.
phone 01772 815629

Availability: Available at farmers' markets across the region and direct to retailers and caterers.

Notes on fruit

It irritates me so much that we have some fabulous, traditional fruits, and yet when the appropriate season arrives, the supermarkets are full of products from countries as far away as New Zealand and South Africa. I don't mean mangoes, kiwi fruit and bananas, but those indiginous to England such as apples, pears and strawberries.

I can understand it, if people want tasteless versions of English fruit out of season, but in season?

The best example of this is blackberries. I remember going to some hedgerow my brother and I had discovered, returning to it patiently, waiting for the berries to turn from red to shiny black, hoping that no one would discover our find and pick them before we did. When ready we would collect some to take home, but invariably ate more than we picked, stuffing our faces with our hands and lips stained 'ribena red' with their juice. Now, in late summer, mums buy them in the supermarket for their kids, neatly sitting on a see through cushioned blanket in a little plastic punnet, mostly imported from Mexico.

If you can resist the temptation of buying out of season, you know it's spring and summer when our traditional fruits are ready. The slightly raspy coarse skin, and the wonderful ripe juiciness of the flesh, like it's hidden underneath and forbidden. Just think of damsons, plums, apples, apricots, blackcurrant, cherries, strawberries, raspberries, gooseberries, grapefruit, peaches, nectarines, pears and rhubarb.

You can tell if a fruit is past its sell-by-date just by looking at it, but you can't tell if a fruit has been picked 'green' and ripened in the air or on a boat, especially when wrapped in plastic so you can't smell if it will taste good. But you can't really go wrong with the local farm that has just picked its own fruit and is selling it in its own shop. You should take the opportunity to see, smell and touch and that will tell you everything you need, to make a buying decision.

Fruit on its own is wonderful, but where would we be without fruit in pies, tarts, puddings, sauces, ice creams and sorbets?

H&P Ascroft

Peter Ascroft
Worthingtons Farm, Park Lane,
Tarleton, Nr Preston,
Lancashire PR4 6JN
phone 01772 814465

Availability: Available to
the trade.

Description: The Ascroft family
have been farming the land
around Holmes in Lancashire
since the turn of the century.
Against the modern trend of
monoculture (growing one crop
only) they have chosen to stick to
the traditional way of growing a
variety of arable crops in rotation
so that the goodness stays in the
soil and pests and diseases are
kept to a minimum.

Chat Moss Herbs Ltd

Colin Brinkman
and Denise Mottram
Barton Moss Road, Eccles,
Greater Manchester M30 7RL
phone 0161 787 8338
www.chatmossherbs.co.uk

Availability: Selected food outlets
including delicatessens and
restaurants, and at food events.

Description: Chat Moss Herbs
specialise in sales of a wide
variety of fresh cut herbs, sold
in 30g packs to 1kg packs.
Also a range of Pesto sauces
and speciality infused oils.
The company is able to pack
products in sizes according
to customer requirements.

Church Farm Organics

Steve & Brenda Ledsham
Church Lane, Thurstaston, Wirral,
Merseyside CH61 0HW
phone 0151 648 7838
email sales@churchfarm.org.uk
www.churchfarm.org.uk

Availability: Farm shop on site.

Description: Winner of four
Organic Food Awards including
"Best Farm Shop", with Soil
Association and Les Routiers
accreditation. There is a delightful
coffee shop and exceptional
cheese counter and they sell a
large variety of organically grown
produce. In addition they also
supply local restaurants.

Flavourfresh Salads

Ray Plummer
Aldergrove Centre,
Marsh Road, Banks, Southport,
Merseyside PR9 8DX
phone 01704 232223
email
ray.plummer@flavourfresh.com
www.flavourfresh.com

Availability: Farmers' markets
and quality supermarket chains,
including Marks & Spencer.

Description: Flavourfresh Salads
specialise in the production of
high quality tomatoes. The range
has developed over many years
to give unbeatable choice in
quality, flavour, shape and eating
experience. They supply to
a range of famous restaurants
and food retailers including
Marks & Spencers.

Kenyon Hall Farm

Tod Bulmer
Kenyon Hall, Winwick Lane, Croft,
Warrington, Cheshire WA3 7ED
phone 01925 763161
email bulmer@kenyonhall.co.uk
www.kenyonhall.co.uk

Availability: Mail order and box
delivery scheme, also own
farmshop on site.

Description: Well known 'pick
your own' and farm shop,
especially for their asparagus,
herbs, strawberries, raspberries,
tayberries, gooseberries,
blackcurrants, redcurrants,
white currants, garden peas,
mangetout, sugar snaps, broad
beans, new potatoes, pumpkins
and squashes. Refreshments and
picnic/play area also available.

The Lakes Free Range Egg Company

David Brass
Meg Bank, Stainton, Penrith,
Cumbria CA11 0EE
phone 01768 890460
www.lakesfreerange.co.uk

Availability: Available from many
food retailers across the region.

Description: Producers, packers
and distributors of quality free
range eggs, produced to Lion
Code and 'Freedom Foods'
welfare standards, which can
be packed in Lakes or 'own label'
packaging. Suppliers to
wholesalers, retailers, supermarkets,
corner shops, farm shops, hotels
and restaurants.

RA Owen & Sons

Julie Owen
Brookfield Farm, Hall Lane,
Simonswood, Nr Liverpool,
Merseyside L33 4XX
phone 0151 548 4611

Availability: Box delivery scheme.

Description: Family farm growing
corn, potatoes, sugar beet and
a variety of vegetables. They also
have a milk round with a box
scheme of quality seasonal
vegetables, the majority of which
are freshly harvested on their
own farm.

W&EF Neale

Freda Neale
The Farm, Martin Lane, Burscough,
Ormskirk, Lancashire L40 0RT
phone 01704 892247

Availability: Available from their
farm shop and at farmers' markets
in Lancashire and Merseyside.

Description: For generations the
Neale family have been farming
in the heart of rural West
Lancashire, with the best of their
traditionally grown vegetables
available at their farm shop and
throughout farmers' markets across
the North West. The family also
make chutneys, jams, pickles
and preserves.

Yew Tree Farm Shop

Graham & Ann Lund
Yew Tree Farm, Lower Road,
Halewood, Liverpool,
Merseyside L26 3UA
phone 0151 487 5165/3273
email shop@yew-tree-farm.org
www.yew-tree-farm.org

Availability: Farm shop on site.

Description: A family run, high class farm shop housed in a recently renovated 17th Century barn. Stocking an extensive range of locally sourced fine foods including fruit and vegetables, preserves, cakes, biscuits, ice cream, eggs, cheese, bacon, sausage and paté. Also home produced award winning burgers, lamb and turkeys.

Notes on herbs

Herbs are always leaves and most likely to be green, with seeds, fruits, pods, bark, stalk and roots being considered a spice. Thank goodness so many of us are using fresh herbs as opposed to dried, which only smell and taste of a feint mustiness to me.

The dried equivalent are sometimes useful but heat and light make them deteriorate very quickly, and when you consider they are usually kept in a hot kitchen in a glass jar exposed to light, they don't last long at all.

The only problem with fresh herbs, is our most convenient outlet is the local supermarket where they are sold at hugely inflated prices - nearly ten times the wholesale equivalent. A stall at a farmers' market can sell a huge fragrant bunch of freshly picked herbs at a fraction of the cost, admittedly only at the right time of year, but it's such tremendous value not just in terms of cost, but taste too.

The herbs that are packed in those plastic cartons with the plastic cellophane topping, are grown quickly, often without soil, using techniques with a long shelf life the most important factor. The basil, mint, chives, parsley, bay leaves, tarragon etc are from Spain, North Africa, Colombia or Israel. That packaging is air tight and generally flushed with gases to stop them spoiling, mostly they will have lost their goodness, especially if they have been washed in chlorinated water which makes them lose their flavour.

The pots aren't much better. The ones you see in supermarkets are usually grown in the UK, but they're grown quickly under artificial conditions, taking easily less than a month from planting the seed to appearing on the supermarket shelf. That's why no matter how you try to look after them, they're pretty much dead after a week. Specialist nurseries and farms grow theirs in soil over the winter. Most will have survived the temperatures and developed a mature earthy flavour. If you can buy at a market or grow your own, herbs are a magical addition to pretty much any fresh meat.

nwfinefood awards
2007

THE Best
OF THE Best

BEST DAIRY PRODUCT
Dew-Lay
Garstang Blue cheese

BEST BAKERY OR CONFECTIONERY
Munx Lakeland Bakery
Cumbrian Honey Bread with Fig

BEST FRESH MEAT
Johnson & Swarbrick
Corn Fed Goosnargh Duck

BEST CURED OR COOKED MEAT
Farmersharp
3 Month Air Dried Mutton

BEST SAUSAGE
Fence Gate Inn
Pork, Leek, Black Pudding and Sage Sausage

BEST FISH OR SEAFOOD
Port of Lancaster Smokehouse
Naturally Smoked Boneless Kipper

BEST BEVERAGE
Millstone Brewery
'Love Saves the Day' Beer

BEST CHUTNEY OR PRESERVE
Lizzie's Handmade
Cumbrian Frutta Cotta Mostarda

BEST PREPARED MEAL
Broughs Butchers Birkdale
Lancashire Hot Pot

nwfinefoodawards
2007

Index OF
NW FINE FOOD
AWARD 2007
WINNERS

The finest food
outlets in the North West

Delicatessens

Farm shops

Restaurants

Cafes

Farmers' markets

Distributors

Demanding local produce

One quarter of all lorries on our roads are carrying food, and almost as much greenhouse gas is created by moving food than by all the power stations in the UK. How did it get to this?

One hundred years ago, practically all the food we ate came from within 30 miles of our homes. If you try to do your weekly shop at the supermarket now, you couldn't choose only local produce, even if you wanted to.

There's no doubt that finding local produce is a time consuming business, you just have to do your research before you can work out how to get really good local food. NW Fine Food has tried to deliver a website (www.nwfinefood.co.uk), that allows you to tap in your postcode and instantly find your nearest producer, farm shop, farmers' market or deli.

However, once that research is done, plus a little bit of trial and error in terms of what suits your taste, and how accessible outlets are, the benefits are huge. You can also plan your journeys so that you become efficient with your time and the energy you use.

When you begin to learn about mass-produced food and how 'economical with the truth', some of these multi-national producers can be, it is truly shocking. How the managers and owners of such businesses can sleep at night, knowing what parents are feeding their children as a result of their advertising campaigns, it's difficult to comprehend.

When you know something about the food you eat, who made it and where it's come from, it dawns on you that you have a role to play in all this. Supermarkets only sell what people buy. Yes, shelf life and cheapness are their main priorities, but if we didn't accept that any more they would respond immediately. We could make a big impact on the environment, surplus packaging, animal welfare and our own health.

NW Fine Food delicatessens and farm shops

What better way to get a real taste of the North West than by paying a visit to one of our many farm shops or delicatessens.

They can range from the very simple 'field to shop' operation to the sophisticated retail experience, which might be better described as a rural or urban deli. Our favourite farm shops are the unflashy family businesses where the owners have occupied the land as long as anyone can remember, and take pride in producing their own fruit and vegetables for you to taste in all their magnificence. Often they will throw in their family produced jams, chutneys, cakes or breads, using recipes that some long lost relative provided. The best delis are those that take huge amounts of time and care sourcing local products, so that we don't have to search for them ourselves.

Al Dente Ltd

Jennifer Hicks
49 Five Ashes Road,
Westminster Park, Chester,
Cheshire CH4 7QS
phone 01244 675994

Description: Chester's fine food delicatessen provides a wide range of locally produced and international food. Products include; continental meats and patés, local cheeses, olives and antipasto, fresh bread, smoked fish, homemade condiments, pasta, oils and vinegars, celebration cakes and hampers. Outside catering service also available at venues within range of Chester

Barbakan Delicatessen Ltd

Victor Hyman
67-71 Manchester Road,
Chorlton-cum-Hardy,
Greater Manchester M21 9PW
phone 0161 881 7053
www.barbakan-deli.co.uk

Description: The Barbakan Delicatessen has over 35 different kinds of bread, baked fresh on the premises every day ranging from Polish Rye, to 'Tomato, Cheese & Bacon Bread'. Also available are freshly made soups and an extensive selection of sandwiches made using their delicious breads (of course) and a mouth-watering range of deli products and continental cakes. Wholesale customers supplied in and around Manchester.

The Cheese Shop

Carole & Malcolm Faulkner
116 Northgate Street, Chester,
Cheshire CH1 2HT
phone 01244 346240

Description: Established in 1985
by Carole Faulkner, the famous
Cheese Shop in Chester
specialises in British foods with a
strong emphasis on local and
Northern produce. The Cheese
Shop also has a wholesale
business with its own refrigerated
transport fleet for trade customers.
Mail order service available.

The Cheshire Smokehouse

John & Darren Ward
Vost Farm, Morley Green, Wilmslow,
Cheshire SK9 5NU
phone 01625 548499
email
sales@cheshiresmokehouse.co.uk
www.cheshiresmokehouse.co.uk

Description: This smokehouse
in the heart of Cheshire produces
a range of smoked meats, fish,
game and nuts smoked on the
premises, together with a wide
range of accompaniments and
complementary fine foods.
There is an award winning café,
a specialist patisserie and a
renowned Fine Wine department.
Winners of the BBC 'Speciality Food
Shop of the Year' 2002, and
numerous other taste awards.
Delivery to local trade.

Chilli Lime Deli

John Caffrey
17 Fleming Square, Blackburn,
Lancashire BB2 2DG
phone 01254 52229
www.chillilimedeli.co.uk

Description: This new and
exciting deli boasts a wide range
of quality, international produce,
including Italian, Greek, Oriental
and Mexican, with a hot chilli
sauce selection that is something
else! There is also good quality,
local produce which is relfected
in the local cheese selection and
speciality pies. Mail order online.

Claremont Farm

Ian Pimbley
Old Clatterbridge Road,
Bebington, Wirral,
Merseyside CH63 4JB
phone 0151 334 1906
www.claremontfarm.co.uk

Description: Farm shop selling
a superb range of fine foods and
local produce; cheese, smoked
meat, home grown seasonal
vegetables including potatoes
and asparagus, seasonal game,
and tickets for the Claremont
Fishery. Also a full range of
seasonal ready picked soft fruits
and pick your own available.
Mail order online.

Country Harvest

Elizabeth Barker
Ingleton, Via Carnforth,
Lancashire LA6 3PE
phone 01524 242223
email info@country-harvest.co.uk
www.country-harvest.co.uk

Description: Quality food retailer,
with renowned coffee shop, craft
and clothing departments. Open
since October 1993 and named
Independent Cheese Retailer UK
in 1999. Hampers are supplied
by mail order or from the shop
- a welcome gift for any occasion.
Stockists of many NW Fine Food
members' products.
Mail order online.

Davenports Farm Shop

Belinda Davenport
Bridge Farm, Warrington Road,
Bartington, Northwich,
Cheshire CW8 4QU
phone 01606 853241
www.davenportsfarmshop.co.uk

Description: Quality farm shop
offering great tasting food which
has been home grown or sourced
locally, and organic wherever
possible. Great service from
friendly and knowledgeable
staff and at reasonable prices.
Diabetic and gluten free
products available. Also flowers
by mail order.

Delifonseca Ltd

Candice Fonseca
12 Stanley Street, Liverpool,
Merseyside L1 6AF
phone 0151 255 0808
email info@delifonseca.co.uk
www.delifonseca.co.uk

Description: Fantastic new deli,
with a vision to provide a
cornucopia of all things foodie
for Liverpool City Centre. A wide
range of English cheese and
charcuterie, breads and fresh free
range eggs. Has recently opened
a restaurant on site serving
anything from simple coffee and
cake to a three course meal.

Dunscar Garden Centre Ltd

Shaun Lewis
106-116 Southport New Road,
Tarleton, Nr Preston,
Lancashire PR4 6HY
phone 01772 811111
email sales@hilaryclare.com
www.hilaryclare.com

Description: This five acre site
offers ample parking and
convenient shopping seven
days a week. Their new espresso
bar serves fantastic coffee and
light lunches, and there is a
comprehensive range of
tableware and gifts for sale.
A wide range of fine foods are
available including smoked foods
from across the North West. They
also make up hampers and offer
local and nationwide delivery
and mail order.

Fir Tree Farm

Alan Abbott
Kings Moss, Crank, St Helens,
Merseyside WA11 8RG
phone 01744 892277

Description: Producers of
vegetables and pick your own
strawberries in season, with a farm
shop on site and a new café.
Fir Tree Farm sells wonderful
home grown seasonal fruit and
vegetables and willow crafts.
The cafe sells quality local and
regional delicacies and they also
conduct farm woodland walks.

Harrisons Bakers and Confectioners

Alan Harrison
5 Queens Court, Sadler Road,
Winsford, Cheshire CW7 2BD
phone 01606 591444

Description: A traditional
bakers and confectioners with
a delicatessen. They produce
fresh bread daily from scratch
using bulk fermented doughs
plus a good range of quality
pies and savouries. There is
a wonderful selection of sweet
confectionery products and
a full range of quality, made
to order sandwiches.

Harvey Nichols

Nicki Swales and Michael Currie
21 New Cathedral Street,
Manchester,
Greater Manchester M1 1RE
phone 0161 828 8879
www.harveynichols.com

Description: Harvey Nichols Foodmarket boasts one of the finest deli counters in the region stocked with some of the best regional as well as international supplies. Combined with a Wineshop and Foodmarket that is devoted to selecting the finest food and wine from around the world - it's an experience not to be missed. Hampers available to mail order online.

Holker Hall

Peter Mathew
Cark-in-Cartmel,
Nr Grange Over Sands,
Cumbria LA11 7PL
phone 01539 559084
www.holker-hall.co.uk

Description: The new Holker Food Hall is a celebration of Cumbrian food and drink and an opportunity for everyone to enjoy their distinctive flavours... especially those produced on the Estate including the famous Salt Marsh Lamb. There are other regional delicacies such as newly baked bread, Cumbrian air dried ham, local cheeses and Morecambe Bay Potted Shrimps.

Honeywell Meats

John & Anthony Gornall
Honeywell Eaves Lane,
Woodplumpton, Preston,
Lancashire PR4 0BH
phone 01772 690271

Description: Honeywell Meats are a traditional butchers, famed for their locally produced meats. There is a wide range of delicious sausages and burgers, and a superb range of barbeque meats in season. There is also a full range of game in season, quality fresh and frozen fish, wines and beers, and a continental deli, including local and continental cheeses, and home cooked meats.

Huntsbrook Farm

Sheila & David Walker
East Lane, Homer Green, Thornton,
Liverpool, Merseyside L29 3EA
phone 0151 924 2727

Description: Established nearly thirty years ago, Huntsbrook Farm and shop provide excellent quality fresh local vegetables, fruit, free-range eggs, local honey, farm cheeses, speciality pickles, sausages, home-cured bacon, gammon and home-cured ham, black pudding, paté, dairy produce and delicious local ice cream. They also sell logs, shrubs and plants when in season, with local delivery available

J&J Graham

Tine Valois
6-7 Market Square, Penrith,
Cumbria CA11 7BS
phone 01768 862281
email enquiries@jjgraham.co.uk
www.jjgraham.co.uk

Description: For more than 200
hundred years J&J Graham have
supplied their customers with
excellent food and wine. Shopping
at Grahams has been a part of
people's life in Penrith for
generations. For those that regularly
holiday in the area, it has become
a family tradition to make a detour
to stock up on the way home.
Suppliers to the trade, but also
hampers by mail order online.

The Harvest Store

Margery Reade
Hopley House, Wimboldsley,
Middlewich, Cheshire CW10 OLN
phone 01270 526292
email mail@harveststore.co.uk
www.harveststore.co.uk

Description: This farm shop, tea
room and Bed & Breakfast is easy
to find, and sells fresh Cheshire
produce including, meat,
vegetables and bread.
Customers can treat themslves
to a light lunch followed by a
delicious home made cake and
a Fair Trade freshly ground coffee.
A Farmers' Market is held here
every second Saturday of
the month.

The Hollies Farm Shop

Philip & Edward Cowap
Forest Road, Little Budworth,
Tarporley, Cheshire CW6 9ES
phone 01829 760414
email
mail@theholliesfarmshop.com
www.theholliesfarmshop.com

Description: The Hollies has
developed through three
generations of the Cowap family
and has grown into probably one
of the best examples of a farm
shop in the county. There is a
comprehensive delicatessen,
good wine selection, fresh flowers
and plants, gifts, Cowshed beauty
products, quality chocolates and
confectionery, and best of all,
excellent customer service.
Hampers available by
telephone order.

Liverpool Cheese Company Ltd

Vickie Anderson
29a Woolton Street,
Woolton Village, Liverpool,
Merseyside L25 5NH
phone 0151 428 3942
email
contact@liverpoolcheesecompany.co.uk
www.liverpoolcheesecompany.co.uk

Description: One of Liverpool's
leading specialist cheese shops
selling artisan cheese and
associated products with a
particular emphasis on British and
local goods. Stocking over 100
different cheeses as well as locally
produced chutneys, chocolate,
seasonings and coffees. Many
cheeses are collected directly
from farms and are matured
on site.

Love Saves The Day

Beckie Joyce and David Mills
345 Deansgate, Manchester,
Greater Manchester M3 4LG
phone 0161 834 2266
email
service@lovesavestheday.com
www.lovesavestheday.com

Description: Atmospheric deli
serving fine food, fine wine
and superb coffee. Own label
produce, including excellent
wines, coffees and chutneys.
Fresh sandwiches and daily hot
specials - dining in, or to take
away - the Sunday brunch is a
must. Outside catering available.

Low Sizergh Barn Farmshop and Tearoom

Alison Park
Sizergh, Kendal, Cumbria LA8 8AE
phone 01539 560426
email
apark@lowsizerghbarn.co.uk
www.lowsizerghbarn.co.uk

Description: The 18th Century
stone barn on this organic dairy
farm is full of speciality foods from
their own farm, from Cumbria, and
beyond. The food in the tea room
is made using ingredients from the
farm shop, and you can watch
the cows being milked every day
around 3.45pm from the tea
room's viewing window. There are
two galleries of gifts and crafts
and a farm trail. Hampers
available by mail order online.

Lucy's of Ambleside

Lucy Nicholson
Church Street, Ambleside,
Cumbria LA22 0BU
phone 01539 432288
email
info@lucysofambleside.co.uk
www.lucysofambleside.co.uk

Description: Lucy's of Ambleside
was born in 1989 through a love
of food and people, it has grown
into all that it is today with a café,
restaurant, outside catering, wine
bar and bistro complementing
this fabulous delicatessen.
Winner of the BBC Good Food
Independent Retailer Award 2005.
Mail order online.

Michael & Laura's

Michael & Laura
Unit D, Indoor Market,
Grosvenor Centre, Macclesfield,
Cheshire SK11 6AR
phone 01625 617996

Description: Well established
food retailer who is a regular
feature of the Macclesfield indoor
market. Selling a range of goods,
Michael and Laura are dedicated
to good service, and constantly
seek to improve their product
offering, favouring quality products
from the North West.

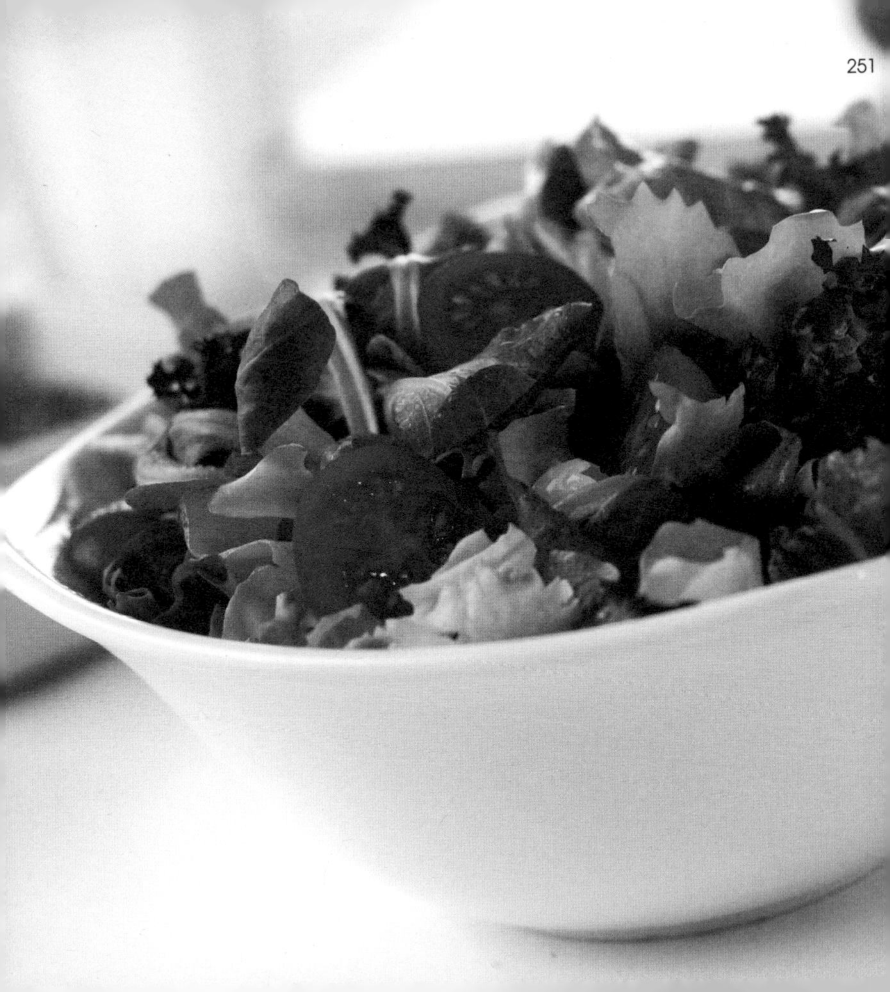

Niche Delicatessen and Café

Debbie Kaye
6 Lower Church Street, Lancaster,
Lancashire LA1 1NP
phone 01524 32333

Description: A new business, Niche are proud to offer a wide range of cheese, charcuterie, breads, wines and fine foods. They are keen supporters of local and regional producers as well as offering a growing range of international products. Their bijou 17th Century building houses a cafe on the upper floor offering excellent teas, coffees, homemade cakes and light lunches.

North Star Delicatessen

Deanna Berlyne
418 Wilbraham Road,
Chorlton, Manchester,
Greater Manchester M21 0SD
phone 0161 862 0133
email info@northstardeli.com
www.northstardeli.com

Description: Chorlton's bright and stylish delicatessen offers superb coffee, home made cakes and savouries as well as a host of fantastic foodstuffs and gift items. North Star also offers a top quality wholesale supply service to food retailers and coffee shops within the Greater Manchester area. Trade deliveries available.

Number 7 Café and Deli

Martin Ainscough and Kate Bristow
7-15 Falkner Street, Liverpool,
Merseyside L8 7PU
phone 0151 709 9633

Description: Café and deli selling
an excellent range of local and
international goods. Well known for
it's homemade cakes and bread
baked at The Station. Wide and
varied cheese selection. An ever
growing range of organic goods
including fresh organic produce.

The Olive Tree

Ged Boardman and Aidan Watts
84 College Road, Crosby,
Merseyside L23 0RP
phone 0151 931 3228

Description: The Olive Tree is
a traditional delicatessen and
coffee shop offering an eclectic
choice of chutneys, preserves,
pastas, ready meals, pies,
quiches, oils, cheeses and
charcuterie. Set in a casual
environment customers can
enjoy a broad range of coffees,
teas and beverages, fantastic
homemade cakes, or choose
from the extensive sandwich
and panini menu.

The Other Place Restaurant and Deli

John Green
121 Allerton Road, Liverpool,
Merseyside L18 2DD
phone 0151 724 1234

Description: The Other Place Deli is situated on Allerton Road serving wonderful products from local suppliers as well as providing 'eating in' and 'eating out' facilities. The finest freshly made sandwiches, paninis and a good selection of local and regional foods from the on site restaurant.

Pelicanos Ltd

Joanna Holt
10 Grovelad Avenue, Hoylake,
Wirral, Cheshire CH47 2DR
phone 0151 633 2680

Description: Delicatessen in Hoylake on the Wirral run by Joanna Holt, serving the local residents with the usual range of regional charcuterie, cheeses, olives, patés and fresh produce.

Redhouse Farmshop and Tearooms

Alan Clare and Jonathan Hewitt
Redhouse Farm, Redhouse Lane,
Dunham Massey, Nr Altrincham,
Cheshire WA14 5RL
phone 0161 941 3480
email info@redhousefarm.co.uk
www.redhousefarm.co.uk

Description: A long established farmshop selling fresh fruit and vegetables, local preserves, specialist cheese, dairy ice cream and some meats including venison. Their 'quintessential' farmhouse tearoom serves light lunches and luxurious homemade cakes everyday. Apple pies and quiches are made each day to take away.

Selfridges

Angela Sawyer, Ian McMullen
and Christian Plumb
1 Exchange Square, Manchester,
Greater Manchester M3 1BD
phone 0161 838 0507
email
angela.sawyer@selfridges.co.uk
www.selfridges.com

Description: Selfridges food halls are an experience not to be missed with regular demonstrations and food counters where you can sample delicious local and international foods. Whether you're a hungry shopper in search of a quick snack or a gourmet chef looking for ingredients, you'll find exactly what you need.

Simply Delicious

Judith Nixon
Cross House, Market Place,
Garstang, Nr Preston,
Lancashire PR3 1ZA
phone 01995 603330

Description: Speciality food
delicatessen, supporting local
producers, as well as stocking
a selection of continental foods,
culinary gifts, a good selection of
olives and artisan breads, organic
wines and spirits and local
handmade chocolates. They also
stock a range of food intolerance
products such as gluten, wheat,
and dairy free.

The Station

Stefan Laprugne
24-28 Hamilton St., Birkenhead,
Merseyside CH41 1AL
phone 0151 647 1047
email info@sleepstation.co.uk
www.sleepstation.co.uk

Description: Café, restaurant and
deli in restored regency building
on the edge of Hamilton Square.
Bread and pastries are particularly
good and made on the premises.
Wide range of organic, locally
produced and international food,
with a couple of meeting rooms
and accommodation.

NW Fine Food farmers' markets and box schemes

Farmers' markets have a strict definition: They can only use that description if the farmers, growers or producers from a defined local area are present in person to sell their own produce, direct to the public.

All products sold should have been grown, reared, caught, brewed, pickled, baked, smoked or processed by the stallholder. It's the reason why we love them so much, because you can actually speak to the person who produced the product and find out all about it. In that way you can be confident you are buying the freshest, local produce possible, supporting your local community and the local economy. In turn, box schemes very often provide the same service, except that they deliver to you. To find out your nearest farmers' market go to www.nwfinefood.co.uk

Ashton-Under-Lyne and Tameside Farmers' and Producers' Market

Ian Kelly and Malcolm Short
Office 10, 2a Henrietta Street,
Ashton-Under-Lyne,
Lancashire OL6 6EF
phone 0161 342 3268
email
malcolm.short@tameside.gov.uk
www.shopatashton.com

Description: The largest farmers' and producers' market in the North West, usually featuring over 70 food stalls, including many NW Fine Food members. Held on the last Sunday of every month, with regular entertainments or demonstrations. NFU North West Regional Winner, Best Farmers' Market Awards 2001.

Fleetwood Farmers' Market

Paul Brown
Adelaide Street, Fleetwood,
Lancashire FY7 6AB
phone 01253 771651
www.fleetwoodmarket.com

Description: Based in the Fleetwood market, one of the oldest traditional markets in Lancashire with over 250 stalls, mostly undercover - the farmers' market is every third Friday of the month, and is well established with a commitment to improving consumer access to local foods.

Manchester Markets

Kendra Kennedy
Manchester City Council,
New Smith Field Market,
Whitworth Street, East Openshaw,
Greater Manchester M11 2WJ
phone 0161 234 7357
email
manchestermarkets@manchester.gov.uk
www.manchester.gov.uk/markets

Description: Manchester Farmers'
and Producers' Market is held
twice monthly, every second and
fourth weekend at 'Piccadilly
Gardens' in the centre of the city
with 21 stalls trading on both
Saturdays and Sundays. Visitors
can buy a wide variety of locally
farmed and produced fresh
foods, including speciality meats,
smoked foods and cheeses.

Northern Harvest

Tod Bulmer
Kenyon Hall Farm, Winwick Lane,
Croft, Warrington,
Cheshire WA3 7ED
phone 0845 6023309
email
orders@northernharvest.co.uk
www.northernharvest.co.uk

Description: Northern Harvest
deliver a full range of really good,
quality local produce direct to
households in the North West.
If you don't have time to go to
farmers' markets, this service can
source top quality supplies from
the best producers and deliver
them weekly. Box delivery scheme
ordered online or by phone.

Rossendale Farmers' Market

Peter Sweetmore
1 Buckingham Close, Helmshore,
Rossendale, Lancashire BB4 4DY
phone 01706 244230
www.rossendalefarmersmarket.co.uk

Description: Monthly farmers
market held on the first Sunday
of each month starting at 10am
in Helmshore, Rossendale (follow
tourist signs to Helmshore Textile
Museum) situated on the edge
of the West Pennine Moors.
Featuring a wide variety of
produce from both local
and regional producers.

Sefton Business Village Partnership

Julie Swarbrick
Pinnacle House, Trinity Road,
Liverpool, Merseyside L20 7HD
phone 0151 934 3441
email
julie.swarbrick@sefton.gov.uk
www.sefton.gov.uk

Description: Sefton Business
Partnership is a private/public
sector initiative, which involves
four partnerships in Bootle, Crosby,
Southport and Altside (Maghull).
The partnerships hold farmers
markets throughout the year in
Bootle, Southport and Maghull,
and are dedicated to bringing
local produce to local people.

Wirral Farmers' Market

Anne Benson
Grove Street, New Ferry, Wirral,
Cheshire CH62 5EJ
phone 0151 643 1393

Description: Wirral Farmers'
Market takes place on the second
Saturday of every month, from
9.00am to 2.00pm, and is run
by volunteers for the benefit of the
community and local producers.
There are currently around 35
producers offering a wide variety
of produce such as beef, lamb,
ostrich, sausages, herbs, fresh
seasonal vegetables, pies, olives
and cider.

NW Fine Food restaurants and cafés

NW Fine Food has a number of 'food service' members across the North West, which includes pubs, cafés and restaurants.

We have strict criteria for membership, but unlike the majority of grading or membership schemes we do not guarantee or pass judgement on the quality of the food served. Instead we verify that these members make every effort to source and use local produce; that they are passionate about the local economy and buying fresh local products because it helps the surrounding community, and actually the resulting dishes taste fresher and more wholesome anyway. Often this commitment takes more time and effort on their part, but we think they should be recognised and you should know who they are.

The Bay Horse Inn (Creation Foods Ltd)

Craig Wilkinson
The Bay Horse Inn, Forton,
Lancaster, Lancashire LA2 0HR
phone 01524 791204
www.bayhorseinn.com

Description: You will find The Bay Horse Inn listed in all the leading restaurant and pub guides. They have also won Lancashire and Lake District Dining Pub of the Year, and 'The Good Pub Guide Lancashire Dining Pub of the Year'. Craig and his team believe in using Lancashire speciality produce and complement the diverse menu with a wonderful choice of wines and real cask ales.

Brasserie Blanc

Jamie Jones
55 King Street, Manchester,
Greater Manchester M24 4LQ
phone 0161 832 1000
email
manchester@brasserieblanc.com
www.brasserieblanc.com

Description: Our aim is simple says internationally acclaimed chef Raymond Blanc "to give the best food, the best service, and value for money". Private dining rooms available for all occasions from family celebrations to corporate events. Various menus are available on request.

Bridgewater Hall

Marco Tedde
Lower Moseley Street, Manchester,
Greater Manchester M2 3WS
phone 0161 950 0018
email
marco.tedde@bridgewater-hall.co.uk
www.bridgewater-hall.co.uk

Description: The Bridgewater Hall is a £42 million international concert hall. It is also a unique venue for conferences, events and banqueting from 10 to 1500 people. It houses the Charles Halle Restaurant and Stalls Café Bar, and was winner of the Manchester Life Restaurant of the Year 2000. Head chef Marco Tedde's food can be described as modern British with French and Mediterranean influences.

Bryson's of Keswick

John Buckley and Paul Carter
42 Main Street, Keswick,
Cumbria CA12 5JD
phone 01768 772257
email
contact@brysonsofkeswick.co.uk
www.brysonsofkeswick.co.uk

Description: Bryson's craft bakery is generally regarded as one of the best in the country for it's quality and range of produce available from it's Keswick Shop and Tea Rooms. The business also supplies speciality items wholesale including finest fruit cake, Lakeland Plum Bread, florentines, shortbread and dairy ice cream.

Burlington's Dining Room and Bar

James Hoole
502 Garstang Road, Broughton,
Preston, Lancashire PR3 5HE
phone 01772 863424

Description: Burlington's Dining Rooms has been trading successfully for over ten years offering the finest local produce, cooked to order using passion, imagination and presented in a unique style. Combine this with a relaxed, professional and unrivalled restaurant atmosphere. Burlington's has a concept that appeals to pratically everyone.

Cariad Coffee House and Tea Rooms

Eirian & Paul Fielding
7 Market Square, Kirkby Lonsdale,
Cumbria LA6 2AN
phone 01524 273271

Description: A warm and relaxed ambience, providing a wholesome and varied menu consisting of locally sourced produce. Handmade and home baked bread and cakes made to their own recipes; the famous Cariad Potato Hash, traditional Sunday roasts, organic seasoned salads, speciality coffees and loose teas, freshly prepared juices made to order.

Conference Centre at LACE

Nicola Hitchen
Croxteth Drive, Sefton Park,
Liverpool, Merseyside L17 1AA
phone 0151 522 1092
www.conferenceatlace.co.uk

Description: An award winning conference centre, beautifully situated on the the edge of Liverpool's Sefton Park. Their chef is passionate about providing creative dishes, whether for a business breakfast, summer BBQ or gala dinner. All food is sourced locally and is freshly prepared each day. They have been awarded the Greater Mersey Food Charter.

The Eagle and Child

Monica Evans
Maltkiln Lane, Bispham Green,
Nr Parbold, Lancashire L40 3SG
phone 01257 462297
email
monica@eagleandchild.com

Description: The Eagle and Child is an award winning country pub on the village green. Selling a wide range of local real ales and high quality food. Extensive use of local ingredients and beef from the owners' farm. Winners of the Lancashire Dining Pub 2005.

Ego Restaurants Ltd

Laura Millar
1a Firemans Square, Chester,
Cheshire CH1 2JA
phone 01244 401501
email info@egorestaurants.com
www.egorestaurants.com

Description: Ego Restaurants are passionate about sourcing the best produce, both locally and from the Mediterranean, including how they select their award winning wines for their wine list. They have fantastic sauces and homemade desserts, and the chefs continually create recipes using local ingredients. Ego has four restaurants in Chester, Heswall, Liverpool and Stockton Heath.

Fence Gate Inn

Kevin Berkins
Wheatley Lane Road, Fence,
Nr Burnley, Lancashire BB12 9EE
phone 01282 618101
email info@fencegate.co.uk
www.fencegate.co.uk

Description: Fence Gate is a beautifully restored three storey 17th Century building. It had been a house to local squires and home of a wealthy cotton merchant, but in 1982 it was extensively modernised with two banqueting suites accommodating up to 400 guests, and a modern brasserie adjacent to the Public Bar. It now has an enviable reputation for its excellent food, fine wines and traditional ales.

Foresight Centre, University of Liverpool

Lynn Westbury and Lesley Dann
1 Brownlow Street, Liverpool,
Merseyside L69 3GL
phone 0151 794 8060
email foresight@liv.ac.uk
www.foresightcentre.co.uk

Description: The Foresight Centre is an award winning business conference centre at the University of Liverpool. Housed within a prestigious Grade 2 Listed building, the centre offers fifteen conference and meeting rooms with state of the art technology. Professional, friendly service combined with catering supplied by an award winning local chef.

The Freemasons Arms

Ian Martin
8 Vicarage Fold, Wiswell,
Clitheroe, Lancashire BB7 9DF
phone 01254 822218

Description: A country pub serving carefully sourced local produce, freshly prepared and served in comfortable surroundings. Award winning wine list with over 500 different selections including cask ales and a large selection of whiskys and brandys.

The Fresh Approach Restaurant

Helen Bent
Bents Garden Centre Ltd,
Warrington Road, Glazebury,
Warrington, Cheshire WA3 5NT
phone 01942 266300
email info@bents.co.uk
www.bents.co.uk

Description: The award winning
Fresh Approach restaurant is
complemented by Caffe Nel
Verde and the Evening Brasserie.
Their team of world class chefs
use only the finest ingredients,
whether it's organic soup with
a choice of speciality breads, a
quick cappuccino or an intimate
four course evening meal.

Garstang Golf Club and Country Hotel

Brian Crewes
Garstang Road, Bowgreave,
Garstang, Preston,
Lancashire PR3 1YE
phone 01995 600100
www.garstanghotelandgolfclub.co.uk

Description: A modern 32
bedroomed family owned hotel
and golf course on the banks of
the River Wyre, with a parkland
golf course and 18 bay floodlit
driving range. The restaurant and
bar serves food prepared from
locally sourced produce. A great
venue for wedding receptions,
civil ceremonies, conferences,
family parties or banquets.

Gibbon Bridge Hotel

Janet Simpson
Chipping, Forest of Bowland,
Preston, Lancashire PR3 2TQ
phone 01995 61456
email
reception@gibbon-bridge.co.uk
www.gibbon-bridge.co.uk

Description: Gibbon Bridge pride themselves on attention to detail and a high level of service for which they have earned numerous awards. Someone once said that staying in a country hotel should be like ´being utterly spoiled in your own home´ and this is what they aspire to achieve. In addition to the great accommodation situated in the beautiful Ribble Valley, there is a restaurant with in-house bakery and conference facilities.

Isinglass Dining Rooms

Lisa Walker and Julie Bagnoli
46 Flixton Road, Urmston,
Greater Manchester M41 5AB
phone 0161 749 8400
www.isinglassrestaurant.co.uk

Description: Voted North West Restaurant of the Year 2005 by Metro News, the 'English Only' menu by owner Lisa Walker won her the prestigious City Life 'Chef of the Year' 2005, and has converted many fans to North West fine food produce. Their commitment to seasonality and local produce is second to none, and they also have meeting rooms available.

The Ladybarn

Kim Merritt
91 Mauldeth Road,
Withington, Manchester,
Greater Manchester M14 6SP
phone 0161 249 3712

Description: The Ladybarn is a recently opened gastro pub in South Manchester. Passionate about good food and drink, the new owners are determined to make the most of local fresh produce and deliver a great service to local residents.

Lakeside Hotel (Yorkcloud Ltd)

Neville Talbot
Lake Windermere, Newby Bridge,
Cumbria LA12 8AT
phone 01539 530001
email sales@lakesidehotel.co.uk
www.lakesidehotel.co.uk

Description: Lakeside Hotel is said to be the best four star hotel in the Lake District. It serves classic and Cumbrian dishes using the finest locally sourced produce, served in elegant surroundings overlooking the lake. The brasserie offers a more contemporary experience, with chic decor and delicious food and the Lakeview Conservatory light meals throughout the day, including traditional Cumbrian afternoon tea.

Langdale Leisure Ltd

Nick Lancaster
and Brian Maidment
The Langdale Estate,
Great Langdale, Nr Ambleside,
Cumbria LA22 9JD
phone 01539 438095
email
nick.lancaster@langdale.co.uk
www.langdale.co.uk

Description: The 35-acre
Langdale Estate is set in the
heart of the English Lake District
in a natural woodland haven
with streams and tarns, dotted with
massive millstones. The Estate
offers a choice of hotel, lodge
and apartment self-catering rental
and timeshare accommodation,
two restaurants, a traditional
Lakeland pub, extensive leisure
facilities plus a health and
beauty salon.

Little Salkeld Watermill

Dave Harris-Jones
Little Salkeld, Penrith,
Cumbria CA10 1NN
phone 01768 881523
www.organicmill.co.uk

Description: Specialist millers
of organic and bio-dynamic
standard flours and cereal
products. For adventurous and
discerning bakers who appreciate
the quality and taste of stone-
ground flours milled the traditional
way, from the best British wheat,
rye, oats and barley. Tearoom,
Millshop and Gallery plus baking
courses, recipes, and an advice
service. Mail order available.

Nectar Restaurant

Jeremy & Jennifer Al-Radhi
12-14 Victoria Road, Hale,
Cheshire WA15 9AD
phone 0161 928 3000
email info@nectarhale.com
www.nectarhale.com

Description: Restaurant serving contemporary seasonal British food, using only local fresh farmers produce, organic and traditional. There are old favourites on the menu such as Shepherd's Pie with Red Cabbage, Anglesey Whiting with Fresh Spinach, Mackerel on Toast, beautiful High Peak Lamb Rump with Roasted Vegetables and lots more.

The Red Pump Inn Ltd

Martina Myerscough
Clitheroe Road, Bashall Eaves,
Nr Clitheroe, Lancashire BB7 3DA
phone 01254 826227
email info@theredpumpinn.co.uk
www.theredpumpinn.co.uk

Description: One of the oldest inns in the Ribble Valley, they have a true passion for using good local produce in their extensive menu in the bar and restaurant at this traditional country establishment where game and local meats feature. Their developing herb garden supplies the restaurant. An on site café and deli sell their homemade bread, cakes and preserves.

The Regent By The Lake

Andrew & Jason Hewitt
Waterhead Bay, Ambleside,
Cumbria LA22 0ES
phone 01539 432254
email info@regentlakes.co.uk
www.regentlakes.co.uk

Description: A family owned and run hotel on the shore of Lake Windermere. The elegant restaurant offers modern English cooking with a 'taste of Cumbria'. Most of the raw produce is sourced locally and their menu changes daily to reflect the seasons. Local seasonal specialities include Lake Windermere Char and local game. AA Rosette for Good Food.

Roses Tea Rooms

Michelle &
Andreas Foulia-Constantinou
23 Milner Road, Heswall, Wirral,
Cheshire CH60 5RT
phone 0151 342 9912
email info@rosestearooms.co.uk
www.rosestearooms.co.uk

Description: Open since July 2005, this remarkable tea room has been a phenomenal success, achieving accreditation into the British Tea Guild. They have also won the Cheshire Life 'Readers Choice' award 2006-7. They only serve high quality food and beverages with most ingredients sourced locally, and everything made on the premises.

RSPB Leighton Moss Nature Reserve

Jacqui Fereday
Silverdale, Carnforth,
Lancashire LA5 0SW
phone 01524 701601
email leighton.moss@rspb.org.uk
www.rspb.org.uk

Description: The Leighton Moss Reserve has a thriving shop and tea room serving both the Royal Society for the Protection of Bird members and non-member visitors throughout the year. The reserve is committed to sourcing produce locally and using Fair Trade and organic options.

Samlesbury Hall

Sharon Jones
Preston New Road, Samlesbury,
Nr Preston, Lancashire PR5 0UP
phone 01254 812010
email
s.jones@samlesburyhall.co.uk
www.samlesburyhall.co.uk

Description: Samlesbury Hall is a 14th Century manor house, recently restored with a fine dining restaurant in The Billiard Room and a number of other rooms suitable for events and conferences. It is a visitor attraction in its own right, with a newly developed kitchen garden that supplies the resident chef with superb home grown produce at its freshest.

Sarah Nelson's Original Celebrated Grasmere Gingerbread

Joanne Wilson
The Grasmere Gingerbread Shop,
Church Cottage, Grasmere,
Cumbria LA22 9SW
phone 01539 435428
email
sarahnelson@grasmeregingerbread.co.uk
www.grasmeregingerbread.co.uk

Description: The Grasmere Gingerbread Shop is unique - it was built in 1630 as the village school and became the home of the truly genuine, Sarah Nelson's Original Celebrated Grasmere Gingerbread in 1854. Today, it is the only place to buy this world famous gingerbread, which is baked daily to a secret recipe.

Tate Café

Bill Smith
Tate Liverpool, Albert Dock,
Liverpool, Merseyside L3 4BB
phone 0151 707 2522
email billsmith@tate.org.uk
www.tate.org.uk/liverpool

Description: Tate Café set within the heart of Liverpool's Albert Dock is an excellent place to pop in for lunch whilst exploring the city's famous surroundings. With a focus on wholesome, local, fresh produce coupled with imagination and flair, Tate Café offers quality food at affordable prices.

The Victorian Chop House Co Ltd

Roger Ward
3 St. Ann's Churchyard,
Manchester,
Greater Manchester M2 7LN
phone 0161 832 1872
email
roger@thevictorianchophousecompany.com
www.samschophouse.co.uk
and
www.tomschophouse.co.uk

Description: Proprietors of Sam's Chophouse in Cross Street, and just across the road, Mr Thomas's Chophouse in Back Pool Fold in the centre of Manchester. Both are atmospheric with tiles, mirrors and timber: evidence of a bygone era. Mr Thomas's is the more pub-like restaurant and Sam's more formal but both serve classic British cuisine focusing strongly on local and regional food.

Weezos Ltd

Kathy Smith and Stosie Madi
The Old Toll House,
1-5 Parson Lane, Clitheroe,
Lancashire BB7 2JP
phone 01200 424478
www.weezos.co.uk

Description: Housed in a Grade 2 Listed building in what used to be the original Clitheroe Toll House, Weezos customers will find an innovative contemporary setting. The menu features modern, simple European cuisine using the best of North West produce. Elegant yet informal Weezos @ The Old Toll House is the newest addition to its two sister restaurants.

Whitewater Hotel

Stewart McIntosh
Lakeland Village, Newby Bridge,
Cumbria LA12 8PX
phone 01539 531133
email
enquiries@whitewater-hotel.co.uk
www.whitewater-hotel.co.uk

Description: Nestling in a valley
on the banks of the River Leven,
which flows from the southern
end of Lake Windermere, the
Whitewater is a 35 bedroom
3 star hotel with extensive on site
leisure facilities. Converted from a
300 year old mill, the Whitewater
has two bars and a riverside
restaurant which uses the best
of fresh, local ingredients.

Lucy's on a Plate and Lucy4

Lucy Nicholson
Lucy's of Ambleside,
Church Street, Ambleside,
Cumbria LA22 0BH
phone 01539 431191
www.lucyofambleside.co.uk

Description: Lucy's on a Plate is
by day a warm and welcoming
informal café experience offering
a range of food freshly made in
their own kitchens, predominantly
from local produce. By night it
transforms into a relaxed candlelit
restaurant. The Lucy4 Wine Bar
and Bistro is in nearby St. Mary's
Lane (phone 01539 434666)
www.lucy4.co.uk

NW Fine Food distributors and trade only

The companies that are involved in distribution and 'trade only' supplies, are really the unsung heroes of the industry, because they're not public facing, and consequently the man in the street has never heard of them.

The ones who are members of NW Fine Food are as committed to local produce and supporting North West producers as our finest delis or farm shops. They can supply local pubs or restaurants with the finest cheese boards, so that they don't need to source them, or they can deliver the best locally produced meat for butchers to turn into fabulous sausages, bacon or your Sunday joint. Their knowledge of the finest NW produce is unrivalled, because they only deal with the best.

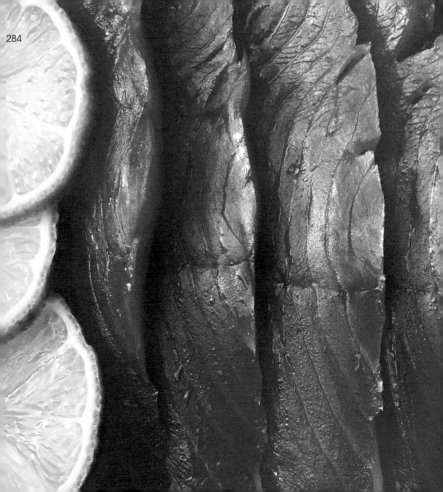

A&H Fine Foods Ltd

Gill & Paul Ackroyd
2 Limbrick Buildings,
Crosse Hall Street, Chorley,
Lancashire PR6 0UH
phone 01257 241332
email sales@ahfinefoods.co.uk
www.ahfinefoods.co.uk

Description: Speciality wholesale distributor of high quality sandwich fillings, cooked meats, soups, cheeses and deli products. The North West's distributor for Innocent drinks and stockists of Feel Good products. Distribution throughout the North West to bistros, sandwich bars, colleges, delis, restaurants and hotels.

Bowland Forest Foods

Jim Curwen
Bowland Farmers Co-operative,
Home Farm Office, Abbeystead,
Lancaster, Lancashire LA2 9BQ
phone 01524 793558
email info@bowlandforest.co.uk
www.bowlandforest.co.uk

Description: Bowland Forrest Foods are committed to providing the highest quality produce, reared on accredited farms by farmers who care. The meat is then handed on to high quality butchers capable of providing a product prepared and packed to the highest standards. Bowland Forrest Foods is dedicated to working with local farmers and retailers providing unparalleled quality and service. A list of the restaurants and hotels they supply are available on their website.

Bowlander Ltd

Carole Jones
Mill House, Long Buildings, Sawley,
Clitheroe, Lancashire BB7 4LE
phone 01200 449833
email carole@bowlander.co.uk
www.bowlander.co.uk

Description: Bowlander is
a Clitheroe based company
specialising in supplying freshly
frozen chopped herbs, spice
purées, chopped spices, citrus
ingredients and flavoured butters.
Formed in 1990 they are
customer focused and supply
large and small food
manufacturers and wholesalers.

Catering Connection

Anthony McGrath
Unit A15,
New Smithfield Market, Openshaw,
Greater Manchester M11 2WJ
phone 0161 223 8811
email
info@cateringconnection.co.uk
www.cateringconnection.co.uk

Description: Catering Connection
can best be described as a food
service company delivering fruit,
vegetables, milk, cream, deli,
dry goods and a comprehensive
range of UK farmhouse and
continental cheeses to hotels and
restaurants in the North West region.
Local produce is their speciality.

David South (Cheese Distribution) Ltd

Christine South
Southdale House, Holloway Drive,
Wardley Industrial Estate,
North Worsley,
Greater Manchester M28 2LA
phone 0161 279 8020
email
mail@davidsouthcheese.co.uk
www.davidsouthcheese.co.uk

Description: Cheese wholesalers and distributors who source British cheeses from the smallest producers to the larger creameries. Also a wide range of continental cheese from Europe and beyond. Customers include retailers, cash and carry operations, wholesalers, caterers and manufacturers.

Dunsters Farm Ltd

Jeremy Mathew and John Clarke
Waterford Business Park, Bury,
Lancashire BL9 7BR
phone 0161 763 7900
email
john.clarke@dunstersfarm.com
www.dunstersfarm.com

Description: A range of the finest chilled products at realistic prices on sale for independent caterers, hoteliers, delis and small supermarkets to use as a one stop shop. Now situated in purpose built premises in Waterford Business Park, they are situated close to the motorway network to deliver throughout the North West five days a week.

Hill's Fine Foods

Adrian Hill and Pam O'Neil
Shay Lane, Longridge, Preston,
Lancashire PR3 3BT
phone 01772 780333

Description: Hill's Fine Foods
is a small family owned business
based in Longridge. Their aim
is to become the premier
wholesale chilled distribution
suppliers of cheese, delicatessen
products and fine foods to quality
caterers and retailers across the
North West and Yorkshire.

Mark Clegg & Co

Janis McLure
Blackburn Road, Longridge,
Preston, Lancashire PR3 2YY
phone 01772 785655
email janis@markclegg.co.uk
www.markclegg.co.uk

Description: Mark Clegg &
Company is one of the region's
premier importers and distributors
of quality chilled foods. They serve
a broad range of trade customers
throughout the North West.
Dedicated to delivering a better
choice without compromising
on quality and value. Service is
a vital ingredient in their business
philosophy. Orders taken by phone.

McKenna's Tender Meat Company

Sean &
Dominique Hebden McKenna
Raby House Lodge,
Benty Heath Lane, Willaston, Wirral,
Cheshire CH64 1SB
phone 07952 703231
email
mckenna.sean@merseymail.com

Description: Winners of a Dept. of Trade and Industry Smart Award, McKenna's produce individually portioned and vacuum packed tender steaks in their chef's unique freshly made marinades. Locally sourced ingredients of the highest quality are used, and are distributed to restaurants, pubs, sandwich bars and delis. Mail order online available soon, phone for more details.

Pendleside Foods Ltd

Rachel Abram and David Tattersall
Glenfield Mill, Glenfield Road,
Nelson, Lancashire BB9 8AR
phone 01282 616826
email
rachel@pendlesidefoods.co.uk
www.pendlesidefoods.co.uk

Description: Pendleside Foods has grown over the years and have built a reputation for supplying high quality products to over 600 outlets throughout the North of England. Much of their range is sourced from small cottage industries that specialise in home recipe and traditional regional products.

Pendrill 1651 Ltd

Loni Papprill
Mollington Grange, Chester,
Cheshire CH1 6NP
phone 01244 851600
email loni@pendrill.co.uk
www.pendrill.co.uk

Description: Regional cheese merchants and distributors of specialist ingredients sourced throughout the North West and other UK regions. Chilled delivery service to chefs and specialist food stores. Collection service direct from producers throughout the region, phone or visit website for more details.

Shlurp!

Lucy Walker
Unit 2, Brazennose House East,
Brazennose Street, Manchester,
Greater Manchester M2 5BP
phone 0161 839 5199
email soup@shlurp.co.uk
www.shlurp.co.uk

Description: Shlurp was founded with the express intention of providing good quality reasonably priced and locally sourced food for local delivery, cooked daily using imaginative recipes. Their food is fast, fresh and great quality with no additives. "Manchester's award winning soup specialist" - City Life Food and Drink 2006.

Total Food Service Solutions Ltd

Graham Sheard
Pendle Trading Estate, Chatburn,
Clitheroe, Lancashire BB7 4JY
phone 01200 441260
www.totalfoodservice.co.uk

Description: Wholesale frozen
and chilled foods, fresh poultry,
fresh meats and provisions.
Suppliers to hotels, delicatessens
and caterers throughout England
and Wales. Temperature
controlled delivery service, with
regular deliveries throughout the
North West to trade customers.

NW Fine Food
Worth a mention

Whilst it is easy to pigeonhole some operations into neat descriptions such as farm shops or farmers' markets, there are other organisations that defy obvious categorisation, but make a significant contribution to the local produce agenda.

Here you will find an assortment that we work with, and who we highly recommend.

A Zest for Food

Brian Mellor
157 Greenwood Crescent, Orford,
Warrington, Cheshire WA2 0EB
phone 01925 498900
email brian@azestforfood.com
www.azestforfood.com

Description: A unique business devised by Masterchef Brian Mellor. Brian is popular as a cookery demonstrator and celebrity chef, well known for his entertaining and informative demonstrations. His company also offers product and menu development, food styling and many aspects of food safety training and consultancy.

Andrew Southcott Catering

Andrew Southcott
Units 6 and 7,
Airfield Approach Business Park,
Flookburgh, Grange-over-Sands,
Cumbria LA11 7LS
phone 01539 559090
email info@outsidecatering.com
www.outsidecatering.com

Description: An outside catering company specialising in weddings, corporate hospitality and outside events, from Royal occasions to product launches, providing a bespoke catering service second to none. Their vehicles have been specially designed to their own specification and are temperature controlled to ensure that the food chosen is kept to the highest standards and can be delivered in perfect condition.

Cooks Corner (Run Cookware)

David Bull
The Coppins, Mortimers Cross,
Leominster, Herefordshire HR6 9TQ
phone 01568 708917
www.runcookware.co.uk

Description: Providers of high
quality, handmade, cast
aluminium cookware with oven
proof handles. A unique ceramic
laminate finish ensures a total
non-stick and non-burn surface.
Ideal for all types of cookers and
all with a 25 year guarantee.
Mail order online.

Dane Stone Cards

David Baxter
1 Danes Howe, Rusland, Ulverston,
Cumbria LA12 8LB
phone 01229 860267
email david@dane-stone.co.uk
www.dane-stone.co.uk

Description: Producer of food
related printed material, especially
postcards with local and
traditional recipes. These cover
Northern counties of England
and have proved popular in
a range of outlets. Dane Stone
also offer a nationwide
commissions service for food
producers and processors,
delicatessens and hotels.

Design A Sausage - Spicetech UK Ltd

Gaynor Preece
and Janet Schuster
12 Hibel Road, Macclesfield,
Cheshire SK10 2AB
phone 0845 257 8884
email
products@sausagemaking.co.uk
www.designasausage.com

Description: Design a Sausage promote home sausage making, using local produce to create gourmet sausages. Their website supplies answers to your sausage making questions and you can order all your supplies and equipment via mail order. They even supply you with their award winning recipes.

Hooray for Home Cooking Ltd

Jill Wadeson
PO Box 456, Preston,
Lancashire PR1 8GG
phone 01772 252131
www.hoorayforhomecooking.co.uk

Description: Hooray for Homecooking are agents for importing and promoting cookery equipment and products, and promoting home-cooking and healthy eating. They are keen advocates of the "remoska" a Czech pan in which you can cook just about anything. They also provide catering for corporate and private events. Mail order online.

Lion Salt Works Trust

Andrew Fielding
Ollershaw Lane, Marston,
Northwich, Cheshire CW9 6ES
phone 01606 41823
www.lionsaltworkstrust.co.uk

Description: Henry Ingham
Thompson's open-pan salt works
closed in 1986. The Lion Salt Works
Trust proposes to restore the site as
a working industrial museum and
funding in the region of £2m is
required. The traditional process
evaporates an unrefined brine to
make coarse, common, and fine
salt without the use of anti-caking
agents and an interesting
exhibition is on site and open
to the public.

Lucy Cooks, Cookery School

Lucy Nicholson
Mill Yard, Staveley, Nr Kendal,
Cumbria LA8 9LR
phone 01539 432288
email info@lucycooks.co.uk
www.lucycooks.co.uk

Description: Lucy Cooks is
the most recent addition to the
Lucy's collection – a fabulous
cookery school based at
Staveley with a fresh and vibrant
approach, where you can be
inspired, educated and above all,
entertained. Whether you are 9 or
99 they offer a range of courses
and demos designed to suit
everyone from novice to Nigella.

Lucy's Inside Out

Lucy Nicholson .
Church Street, Ambleside,
Cumbria LA22 0BU
phone 01539 432223
email
insideout@lucysofambleside.co.uk
www.lucysofambleside.co.uk

Description: Lucy's of Ambleside
now has a dedicated outside
catering unit that can cater for
everything from delicious dinner
parties through to weddings
and special celebrations – from
an intimate dinner for two, to a
large scale celebration for 200.
They have a range of menus that
are guaranteed to excite the
taste buds – from a 'Feast on
the Fells' picnic menu to a
'Centrepiece Buffet'.

Manchester Merchant Wines

Jon Croft
Market Court,
20-24 Church Street, Altrincham,
Cheshire WA14 4DW
phone 0161 877 4680
email info@merchantwines.co.uk
www.merchantwines.co.uk

Description: With a portfolio of
over five hundred wines,
Manchester Merchant specialise
in original and exclusive Italian
wines and provide superior service
to complement their superb wines,
giving the personal touch with
every order. Ideal if you require a
gift, would like a tasting event or
just wish to increase your private
wine collection. Mail order
available through phone orders.

We think our three
Food Lovers Festivals
are the best foodie
events in the region,
and the 35,000 visitors
they attract each year
seem to agree.

nwfinefood

lovers festivals

Each event features around 80 fine food producers and an exciting programme of celebrity chef demonstrations, producer talks and children's entertainment, to keep you occupied between eating all those samples. You'll find a great mix of cheese, ice cream, chutneys, puddings, chocolate, beer, jams, pastries, breads, oils, liqueurs, olives, traditional soft drinks, fish, hams... well, you get the idea.

16th and 17th June 2007
Westmorland
County Show Ground
near Milnthorpe, Cumbria
Brian Turner
and Steven Doherty

11th and 12th August 2007
Stonyhurst College
near Clitheroe, Lancashire
Gino D'Acampo
and Nigel Haworth

27th and 28th October 2007
Tatton Park
Knutsford, Cheshire
Jean-Christophe Novelli
and Simon Rimmer

Entrance 11am to 5pm
(with last entry at 4pm)
each day.

Pay on the door
or visit www.nwfinefood.co.uk
to buy tickets online.

Index
OF
NW FINE FOOD
MEMBERS

Index
OF
NW FINE FOOD
MEMBERS

Index
OF
NW FINE FOOD
MEMBERS

Index
OF
NW FINE FOOD MEMBERS

Index
OF
NW FINE FOOD MEMBERS

Index
OF
NW FINE FOOD
MEMBERS

Index
OF
NW FINE FOOD
MEMBERS

Honest local food, laid bare

We can't afford television advertising, flashy food stylists, airbrushed photographs, expensive packaging, sultry voiceovers, caramelised advertising executives or unnecessary preservatives, colourings, flavourings and additives.

To tell you the truth, we don't want to, anyway.

What we make is often the result of generations of work - recipes handed down, animals looked after, fruit and veg lovingly cared for. If you talk to our producers they're open and honest about the way they create the end product, and that's how we like it. The big boys might have hijacked all the marketing phrases but if you rely on your senses, you really can smell, see and (ha ha) taste the difference.

We need more support in the fight to get the public to buy local produce to cook at home, to demand it in restaurants or ask for it in supermarkets. Give us a hand to give the marketing big spenders a run for their money by becoming a NW Fine Food Lover member. Visit www.nwfinefood.co.uk and find out how.